Goldengrove

LORNA GOODISON was born and grew up in Jamaica, and she now teaches in the Department of English and the Center for African and African American studies at the University of Michigan. Her many honors include the Commonwealth Poetry Prize (Americas Region), the Gold Musgrave Medal from Jamaica and the Henry Russel Award from the University of Michigan. Her work, which has been widely translated and anthologised, appears in the *Norton Anthology of Modern and Contemporary Poetry*.

D1354411

1 1 0564817 1

Also by Lorna Goodison

Tamarind Season (Institute of Jamaica, Kingston, Jamaica 1980)

I Am Becoming My Mother (New Beacon Books, London 1986)

Heartease (New Beacon Books, London 1988)

Selected Poems (University of Michigan Press, Ann Arbor 1992)

To Us, All Flowers Are Roses (University of Illinois Press, Urbana and Chicago 1995)

Turn Thanks (University of Illinois Press, Urbana and Chicago 1999)

Guinea Woman: New and Selected Poems (Carcanet Press, Manchester 2000)

Travelling Mercies (McClelland & Stewart, Toronto 2001)

Controlling the Silver (University of Illinois Press, Urbana and Chicago 2005)

LORNA GOODISON

Goldengrove

New and Selected Poems

CARCANET

First published in Great Britain in 2006 by
Carcanet Press Limited
Alliance House
Cross Street
Manchester M2 7AQ

Poems from *Travelling Mercies* used by permission of McClelland & Stewart Ltd.
First published by McClelland & Stewart Ltd., Toronto, 2001

Poems from *Controlling the Silver* published by arrangement with
the University of Illinois Press. All rights reserved. First published in the United States
by the University of Illinois Press, Urbana and Chicago, 2005

Controlling the Silver is available from Marston Book Services, Ltd.,
160 Milton Park, PO Box 269, Abingdon OX14 4YN, United Kingdom

A CIP catalogue record for this book is available from the British Library
ISBN 1 85754 848 5
978 1 85754 848 8

The publisher acknowledges financial assistance from Arts Council England

Typeset by XL Publishing Services, Tiverton
Printed and bound in England by SRP Ltd. Exeter

Contents

from *Controlling the Silver*

New Poems

Balm

On love lane, the chemist and dispenser
changes each day into a fresh clean gown
and from every corner of way downtown
the lovestruck come to buy his essential oils.
Oil of hold, oil of keep and never leave.
And what substance could that be that binds so?
What unguent with fragrant scent that remains
on the skin and coats the hairs of your head
so that your every thought triggers a rush
of aromatic atoms, and your love comes
to prefer your scent above all, and absent
from the valleys of your strong smells calls
for the cure of your salt sweat like medicine?
Need you. Need you like bluestone and sulphur
need a stubborn ulcer. Balm me Beloved.

I Come From a Land

I come from a land
where the same shop
offers morning breakfast,
dressmaking and fish.

Where the port of St Mary
is inscribed in Spanish
and called in the tongue of Twi.

Where a signboard
basted with words
reads: Essie's establishment
of dressmaking, good work dun
sew to fit all sizes
no weapon that is formed
against me shall prosper.

Essie say the water cold
the canoe cannot go forth
for fish take low and gone deep.
No fish today, try greens.

No weapon that is formed
against you shall prosper.
You yourself form no weapon.
Go deep when water cold,
there do your good work,
but only Essie can fit all sizes.

On Leaving Goldengrove

A letter and seven notes inspired by a narrative from W.H. Hinson

Dear Cousin Margaret,

Yes, what you hear is true, I am now apprentice to Cassamere

who was brought to Goldengrove for the express purpose
of blending fine liqueurs for one Mrs Christian Henry.
O Cassamere, he is a master of at least five trades.

For in between pressing pineapples and coffee berries
to make rude-to-parents drinks, he found the time
to renovate Reverend John Smith's old wereketty carriage.

And this, cousin, is what caused me to leave Goldengrove.

For I stopped to stare in wonder at the transformation
wrought by the hands of a master: the gold burnished
side panels, the artfully laid down cushions of velvet,

the perfect and so regular disc of the balanced wheels.

My open admiration caused my heartless stepfather
to have my feet placed in stocks for neglect of duty
because I stood and wondered at the work of Cassamere

who is also a master and born promoter of the dancing trade.

Such a farewell dance he held there at Goldengrove!
with skilled musicians brought in from Kingston,
Robert Michaels first violinist, one Poly Levy on bass,

a Mr Brissman on trombone and John Cooke clarinettist.

There was also a second and a third violinist, and one big lavish
more-of-plenty dinner provided in accompaniment.
Cousin Margaret, we eat so till we could eat no more.

Yes, what you hear is really true, I leave Goldengrove

with Cassamere who departed with two horses and two carts,
one packed with dry goods, the other transported him,
Amanda Jackson, Sarah Ritter and her little nephew Judah.

I decide my mind to follow him to the ends of the earth.

So me and Benjie Clark followed behind his carriage on foot
all the way to Kingston where I'm now living two doors down
from the residence of Cassamere. Here I am most contented.

Cousin Margaret do not grieve on my leaving Goldengrove.

★

i

What of His Appearance?

What of his appearance?
                              I tell you of his appearance.

A big tall man; strapping and black-skinned.
His is a black so true it holds all colours in it
but favors above all, blue, so his complexion
takes a shine to it: his brown eyes are set deep.

The philoprogenitive organs at his neck back
is a sign, some say, that his nature is strong.
There is nothing that brings him more delight
than to sweetmouth and romance a woman.

He is a dandy who can dress sharp as a tack
always in bespoke black suits and white shirts,
People say he is a native of France or Haiti,
of his nationality he says 'Je suis le roi soleil.'

★

Master of Five Trades

For the proverbs say whatsoever thy hand
findeth to do, thou must do it with all
thy might: for every finger on one hand
Cassamere can count a trade mastered.

For this one man is a restorer and scene
painter, fireworks maker, liquor blender,
a baker and confectioner, besides being
Kingston city's tip top dancing master.

Skilful he is in instructing every movement
of the dance, especially the grand chain,
the five figure quadrille and the stately waltz.
I follow him in the hope of catching a spark

from the great wheel that drives his works,
For to do even one thing well and that with
your all and your might, is the true reason,
philosophers say, that we are given life.

★

iii

A Dancing Master

Where Haywood Street
touches Chancery Lane,
and Orange Street and
Beckford Street meet,
where King Street
connects with Barry Street
Papa Cassamere draws them.
Come one come all.

O cousin come to town
come know what we call
original dance hall.

Pampampalam
         this ya man a man
Ai Zuzuwa
         when him talk no dog bark.

If you see him ride
the rhythm
never out of step
or overstepping
beat obey him.

Just so him hold
a pretty gal
around the waist
against his chest,
when her heartbeat
answer his
that is it
she is his.

The city is filled
with dancing women
changed
into devotees
of Cassamere.

★

iv

The One Man Cassamere Ever Called Master

An old French scientist I did not know
a learned man called Old Prico, was
the one man Cassamere called master.
It was Prico who tipped him moneygifts
as encouragement to sweeten labour
when he saw how God bestowed on
one black man five talents to trade with.
And trade he did, till one day he could
count in his hand two thousand dollars
that he used to buy himself out of slavery
before 1838 the year of general full free.

v

Fireworks

Old Prico is who taught Cassamere this explosive science.
The first time I witnessed his skill at commanding fires
to form pictures, was in a grasspiece at Charles Levy pen,
in the center of which was set a one-room brick house.

First he sent up balloons big as the bellies of elephants.
The crowd breathed deep and trained their eyes
upon them roaming across the skies waterholes.

Don't watch that, watch this!

For then he rolled the fiery wheels, then he caused
sparkling waterfalls to quench fireballs, the stars threw
down their spears from the heavens over Blue Mountains.

He rewired black holes that shone forth like in the ages
when they were fully occupied by our sky guardians
who had looked down and seen those wicked ships
and descended to crouch with us on our rough passage.

We flew flags of all nations all of the same equal size,
cut and carved up darkness with new style lamps
that poured down their gold upon us as reparations
till every upturned face was washed in contentment.

That night Kingstonians went home to tenements,
lay down to sleep, and the ancestors dreamed them,
blessed and assured them, that what they had seen
was but a glimpse of the paradise waiting for them.

In the making of these signs and tokens I assisted,
grinding and firming powder and charcoal, I rolled
sulphur and brimstone, sifted sand, and blended
bright powders to colour our man-made wonders.

When all festivities were done I was put in charge
Of making sure that all stray fires were controlled.
I was then appointed watchman of our equipment
Which I guarded with my life in that brick one-room.

Cassamere came driving a horse and cart at dawn,
with him was a woman in a pink satin evening gown.
I smiled at them both and murmured not one word
for though me poor soul, spent that dark night alone,

it seemed to me as I passed through that straight
and narrow door, that the morning sky overhead
was glowing, stained, with signs and wonders I had
helped the great man, my master himself, to create.

★

vi

A Liquor Maker and Confectioner

The Hidalgos of Hidalgo's Drugstore
were Mr Cassamere's bosom friends
it is for them he made liquors, cakes
and confectionary. You should see him
ice the white tower of a wedding cake
then decorate it with edible ornaments
of silver! He taught me to make marzipan
by crushing almonds in a stone mortar
with a marble pestle; he instructed me how
to boil sweets with peppermint and aniseed
and wrap each in squares of tissue paper
upon which he'd script saucy messages
in his perfect fist: 'candy kisses', 'sweets
for the sweet','a kiss from you is bliss'.
Everyone, especially the girls of Kingston,
craved his candy; sometimes I'd carry
a pocketful and scatter some in the streets
just to see the schoolchildren scramble.

★

Last Act of The Restorer and Scene Painter

O cousin Margaret, the night before last
Mr Cassamere was brought home
to his residence above Hidalgo's drugstore.

We bore him through the streets on a stretcher
from the railway where he was employed
to renovate coaches; in the restoration of which,
as is known to one and all, he has no equal.

His last act was to straighten a warped door frame.
He stepped through it, he lay down his tools.
He look a fit, we took him home, this morning he died
in his room hung with sceneries he himself painted.

Glory be to God for his life.

He did not hold back from me one secret of the trades
except the smooth way of the sweet-foot dance master.
That one cousin, not even Cassamere could transfer,
for I was never a one who could limber light on my feet.

Four trades cousin, four to trade with.

Fall Away Iron Filings

What iron filings collect in our hearts
                    Antonio Cisneros

Fall away now iron filings
cross threads across my heart.

Swallowed first
as bitter pills
that in body heat
smelted into chinks of iron.

Weigh down they weigh
my good intentions.
Fire my tongue to curse
when I need spark to bless.

Function as
bearing beams
for rust memories
of canker worm
and locust years
best written off,
yet reinforced by iron
which should be
but pepper dash;
burn in the blood
then gone.

To the ironmonger
god of old iron

your work here is done,
solder on.

Come swiftly love my man of war.

Where I Come From

Where I come from,
old women bind living words
across their flat chests,
inscribe them on their foreheads,
and in the palms of their hands.
If you don't have the eye
to you they just look like
third world women with nothing much.

Under their clothes
on white calico belly bands,
they have transcribed ancient texts
which soak into their stretched loins;
and when they seek cures for you,
their whitlow fingers braille-read
medicine words
from the base of their bellies.

In Dreams of Shipwreck

It is night in the city from which I set out,

here it is morning.

Hear a prediction brought by the waves:

today someone in prison
will turn from thieving
and begin to reclaim swamp land.
After seven years, this ex-thief
rejoicing, will bring in the sheaves.

Now a window opens in the sky
a gang of schoolchildren birds
clamber over the cloud sill.

I need to write into being,
a praise-based constitution
for the grace government
of the rock which smashed
my folly boat to pieces.

A grateful remembering comes
on wings of schoolchildren birds.

A meal of curried chickpeas
cooked by Kamal in Guyana,

Mint tea sipped from a glass
with friend Ali in a Cairo bazaar
before I was allowed to buy
a suitcase of buffalo hide.

Anything sweet or bitter
I received from your hands.
Billow now bright sails of thanks.

The Selflessness of Salmon

From one to five years in the open sea
where salt agrees with sweet flesh
they swim silver delicious pink red.

Then something in the ones who missed
line and net, perhaps a petit mal seizure,
causes them to spasm mid-swim
into remembering waves.

They leave off leaving themselves
free for us to catch,
eschew the loose waterweeds,
and turn with determined grace
for their place of birth.

Bowed, they cross the line
where salt water
parts company with fresh,
re-entering amniotic space
firm flesh settles into soft.

Jumpy, as they wait for upwash tide
for sex urge that brings them death,
she to bring forth red eggs,
he to fertilise them into life,
this their last great giving
before they lay down themselves
for birds and beasts to come
gorge upon selfless salmon.

Naming of Flowers

Honeysuckle: because it perfumed
the front room where she woke
at aged two one Easter Sunday.

No one told her the name, she called it that
for bee-spit honey and breast-milk,
white flower foam from a round vase.

Asters bought in Saturday markets,
shook their shaggy heads in full baskets
of legumes called locally 'leggins'.

They stood for a week in watered vessels
in small rooms with cedar board floors
burnished with coconut brushes.

Brides carried bouquets, most often lilies,
open as the hearts of brides themselves
for whom her mother sewed dresses.

A town child knows little of flora,
but in her grandparent's country garden
every manner of bloom ran riot.

Up the privet walk to the wooden house
flagged row upon row of hibiscus,
red scarves crushed to black shoes.

Beside the tombs in the ancestral
burying ground, a flareup of blue irises
set down as bulbs to brighten

the vault of her uncle murdered
with a sharp edged stone. Irises
brought home by his sister Rose.

To the Buddha Go the Roses

You snip them five stems down
just ahead of high-chest deer
with their penchant for rose moisture.

You bring buds indoors
gold, crimped pink at the edges
and arrange them in a tall vase

where they unclench.
Then on brink of fade, open wide
in full blown ejaculation of thanks.

You take this fallen offering
to the statue of Guatama Buddha
seated in the side garden

at his feet a new mulched bed.
Yellow petals fill stone rice bowl,
you turn your yellow head
and bow slow.
Smiles the Buddha.

Gates of Ivory, Gates of Horn

Can I receive dreams by the same gates
as the ancients? Or are there entrances
and exits marked for the ones like us?

Gates of horn, guarded by the patriarchs
or them who aspire to be, where I am from,
what is horn? We make more of solid-milk ivory

and prize its long-tooth form for being able
to withstand being so outstandingly awkward.
So alone with all its other big friends gone.

So roped into circuses to perform tutu dances
when all it wants to do is trumpet and eat greens.
But this is about my dreams of late, my corpse-

carrying, brushing-off-tombs, being relegated
to ramshackle blue houses dreams. The ivory key:
in my country, to dream of your own death is good.

House being outer shelter, the Beloved must break
and enter to rebuild your essence. Praise then
to dreams of ruined house and grass about tombs.

The news is today is, I come, I go, through this gate,
lift that latch, guard Sweeney, here I pass.

The Lion and the Gypsy Revisited

So, you crowbarred the trapdoor to sleep,
certain the lion in you would emerge
to rage rampant as she lay down to rest
on plain rough sheets of sand, dressed
in her striped dress, the round-bellied
lute-alike flung so careless by her side.
What came sneaking up the sleep passage
was a yellow brindle-puss.

While the rest of the world slept you clawed
her name into the bubbling trouble flame
and cooked up a scheme to rob her of her song,
claimed she had weapons of mass destruction,
then used that as pretext to invade and ransack
the contents of her bag.

But another dream thief in your crowd is out for you.
If I were you I would creep quietly away from there,
follow the sun and catch the first camel-train home.
Learn some manners and wait your turn.
You cannot? You must!

Silence Before Speech

Enter the Bamberg rider.
What he saw turned him
and his mount to stone.

The Arawak grasped Columbus' sword,
watched blood stripe the blade
and uttered no sound.

The heretic who broke
the sphinx's nose was mum
as he marred what man worshipped.

When your idol's nose is broken
it only has eyes for the rose;
kiss-shape your lips; now breathe in and out.

Silence let in can purify and change,
it does its work by visiting each cell
leaving calling cards of scent.

Here a bloom has been,
it faded, then powdered to ash,
extract sweet oil from that, and make balm.

Rub it on in silence: now speak.

Yet Once More I Will Shake

Ah, I should say nowt and nought,
nuttin and nothing.
You have grievances with me, I have
none with you, it is best to let
this be settled by higher arbitration.

What do you want though?
What is it exactly that you want?
My eyes or my eye?
My song or my songs?
How can you have them
you who won't take a chance?

It was like this: I was held in the grip
of I know not what, except that it was
a shaking to and fro, such a shaking
yet once more.
Like some poor soul
who gets picked on
by whirling ones insisting
'wake up' 'wake up'

so that I had to flee within;
and papa what a mashallaw!
I can't even try to tell you
because you really have to
shake for yourself.

I will say this though, it's been decades
and the idols in my living room
are still being overturned.

So having my eyes or eye
is not going to help,
you yourself have to take shake up.

Some time during,
you get used to the maracas clack
of the bones in you
being pitched and tossed

while you eye's eye becomes
fastened down,
but you have to be stirred and shaken.

Rock of Ages

Come Sunday she sits straight-backed
adjusts her gold-framed spectacles,
sight reads and plays the pipe organ
for common prayers who whisper behind her back,

but never to her face set like flint.

Whisper about her husband and who and who
he had lain careless with, but never to her face.

Married in 1910 to a man who rode a white horse
up to her father's door and respectful asked for her hand.

How to know that in addition to land willed him
from an overseer father, he'd inherited too,
the loose way of the busha: a wife at home
and young bush maids picked for easy concubinage.

Let the water and the blood
from her wounded side which flowed...

The Cruel Room

This is the crewel room, not because of the cruel things that happen there
but because of the embroidery
Rose Hall tour guide

With a straight face the guide tells us this.
She tells us some other strange things too,
like how that was a ship-on-dale chair.
Face it, our minds and tongues cannot agree
with some ideas and images in English.
Besides, the original furniture is gone,
removed to the stately home of one of the twenty-one
families who for the most part owned this island.
What we are being shown looks like an eclectic
grouping of all things from mahogany to deal.
We now regret paying one thousand dollars Jamaican
to visit Annie Palmer's renovated mansion
where she is alleged to have murdered
many lovers and husbands in these cruel rooms.
Let us depart from this great house of wickedness;
and go out in haste past her alabaster tomb
from which said guide claims her spirit goes and comes,
no doubt disguised as a rich widow tourist
who invites Montego Bay beach boys, disciples of sex,
to come up and see her at Rose Hall sometime.

What Happened to Peter

Nine days after the killings
he appeared at the front door to ask
'Can you tell me what happened to me?'

I told this to a friend who said
'That means we must remember him.'

So I sing to myself his uplift anthems;
they rise up like incense.

My impression of him was
he was a shy man,
private behind those shades
he never took off.
Between him and everyone else
he maintained a wall of smoke.

The dangerous stepping razor,
oracle who spoke through veils,
spoke a beautiful patterned language.
He decorated, he said, he decorated Bob's music.

Initiate of the order of bush doctor,
who declined all invitations to finnerals
straight singing ginneral,
this I know:
what took him down was twisted.

At the door, I had no answer for him
but hope that I managed to say
something like: thank you Peter Tosh
for helping us get up stand up.
As I watched him step off
rolling lambsbread into blunt,
wherever he lives now, what a music.

Giovanni Paulo

I liked the look of the Pope's face.
He had a kind countenance
burnished by much contemplation.
the kind that cleans your skin.
I don't mean arcane rituals
veiled by smoke from censers,
more the wash of the words 'have mercy'.

They said the Pope prayed fervently
for hours and hours without ceasing
and that in every woman he sighted
the Virgin Mary; therefore
as bearers of the Virgin's DNA
women must remain humble and chaste
surrender control over their own temples
and assume their place below men.

That is what he believed.
I do not believe that.

In fact I say 'fire for that'.

What I liked about the Pope was:
his washed countenance,
the fact that his real life story
read like an epic novel,
and that they buried him in a plain pine coffin
with his scuffed brown working man shoes on.

Abraham and Isaac After

Some weeks after, Abraham invites Isaac
To go with him for their usual evening walk.
Terrified, the child runs and hides.
At least once a week from an early age
Abraham had taken him across the desert
up into the dry brush hills to survey the land.
There they would eat dates and raisins
while he recounted to the boy old tribal stories.

But after the incident:
the boy busies himself; goats to tend to, water
to fetch, he will go so far as to help the women
weave cloth, anything to avoid being alone
with his own father. For ever after he will carry
the image of himself, arms trussed back, face
down on the altar and the suspense of the silver knife.

A Praise Song to Mandiba and the Camphor Trees
of Vergelegen

Start Up Stanza (to be discarded once the poem begins):

What, you wonder will your last image be?
The face of your son, your parents, your dear companion.
The Blue Mountains seen at 6:45 from the vantage point
Of the traffic lights outside King's House?

Or:

The great camphor trees of Vergelegen.

Admit it, the worship of ancestors makes you primitive.

O but you who did not see them should see
their venerable grey trunks come down from the sky
to stand their ground so you must look up to them.

Here an unseen hand tips a candelabra, so a flash
of hot wax sprays us with spitfire blessing

before

Mandiba stands and addresses and chants praises
to Walter Sisulu man of excellence, Peace O Peace be on him.
And the land around which could have run red,
is redolent instead with Mr Nelson Mandela's presence.

(Who was with him when he trampled the winepress;
for he did not trample alone; and if you were there
then your garments are stained with victorious dyestuff
so at this point you too can praise:

Here a wide cloud cloth spreads over Table Mountain,
and Winnie is caught up in its folds of compassion.
She descends from the slope with shining face.

Praise to the laughing man calling out 'I am happy,

happy to have been proven wrong, I who was raised in this place
and left in despair saying the old order never would change,

say fill your cups and drink to the New South Africa and to my
                                                            mistake.'
Praise to Mrs Rabinovitch, bearer of Nelson Mandela's Sunday
                                                            dinner.

Praise to Mandela's cell on Robben Island, a laboratory
where a new human being
was cultured over twenty-seven years,

and here I could just write a line like 'Africa, I love you Africa',
write that and feel not one bit self-conscious
or embarrassed to see camphor trees as ancestors
who tonight breathe down balm on us

for the Soweto String Quartet is putting fiddle to bow
and O my love we the people must rise up once more, and dance.

Windrush Sankey

I come in my one dark serge suit
built for me by my uncle the tailor.

My very best white shirt and merino
washed by my mother in the river

and spread out flat on a shale rock
to be dried by the free heat of the sun.

I come with my stingy-brim felt hat
pushed way back on my head back

where my mother's hands cupped
my head upright, I her one so so son.

And because my parents were born
and are bound to die as canecutter

and grassweeder there in the fields
Of tough blood-at-root stalks of cane

I must leave my village called Albion
without one chance for advancement

but the possibility of some hard food
eaten night and morning with praise.

I come carrying my big cardboard grip
with my other clean shirt and trousers,

my change of underwear, and a quart
bottle of whiterum to sprinkle as I go

from all my people who love me, who
know my full name and who would not

let me die of hungry and cold in a room
without even a shilling for the gas meter.

I wear this my clean shirt and merino
like the big breastplate of righteousness

for my mother sang 'To Be a Pilgrim'
as she ironed them then watched me

put them on to go, away to the harbour
where I then boarded the great ship which

bore me across the wide water to this land
England, land I must now make my home.

from

Travelling Mercies

Spending the Gold of Lovers

Pearl morning, when the Blue Mountains
contracted and stamped themselves, imprimatur,
across your forehead. You witnessed the seal
in the mirror as you combed your hair.

By sun hot, words began to issue from your lips,
words for which you had no meaning like 'Lailah'
which means 'a night,' and 'Ali' who later became
your rose seller.

Like dusk, the rain of coins fell, downpouring
from vents in the ceiling. Gold you gather
and spend freehand, careless and wanton
in your sojournings.

Come winter, a wine-bibber on the number 5 bus
is inviting anyone who so desires to dine with him.
'Anyone who wants to can come, I have money,
I can pay.'

The same gold rain was falling down,
leaking out from the vault of his rented room,
lining his pockets so he became profligate
deaf to the warnings

of the saved and reasonable woman cautioning
'put away that money for rainy days.'
'No,' he maintained, 'I can pay, I will pay,
and whosoever will may come.'

Travelling Mercies

are what we petition
as we row in rough barks
walk foot, or wing

in silver gaulins.
Approaching Castries,
send travelling mercies.

Call them down
for anxious traveller
homing to old mother

herself travelling
in small Morne room
en route to mansions.

Sanction this request
and swift send
journey mercies.

And you, away
from new husband,
brood over Caribbean,

keep us on this voyage
to union,
send down travelling mercies.

What We Carried That Carried Us

I

Song and Story

In ship's belly, song and story dispensed as medicine,
story and song, bay rum and camphor for faint way.

Song propelled you to fly through hidden other eye,
between seen eyes and out of structure, hover.

In barks of destruction, story functioned as talisman
against give-up death, cramped paralysed darkness.

Remaining remnant tasting all of life, blood, salt,
bitter wet sugar. Ball of light, balance power,

pellucid spirit wafer without weight, ingested,
taken in as nourishment, leaven within the system.

Remnant remaining rise now.

II

Dance Rocksteady

You danced upon the deck of the slaver *Antonia*
named for the cherubic daughter of sea captain Fraser.
Aye kumina.

You moved just so, in and out between wild notes
sounded by the suicide followers, staying well within
rock steady rhythm,

range of Kilimanjaro, length of river Limpopo.
Respond again to higher rimshot and one drop
ride rocksteady.

The Living Converter Woman of Green Island

The living converter woman of Green Island
sings in morning as she passes through the valley
'Farewell Night Angel.' She's on her way to the butcher shop,

all the verdant valley ringing
with coloratura converter singing.

Last week she received revelation as she bent over
the tinnin bucket, turning intestines inside out,
shedding the green grass waste of the cow and the goat.

She has turned at least twenty million feet
of tripe on the sceptre of her tripe stick.

Tripe is not straight so. Like all to do with history
long story and memory, it is coiled and sectioned.
Here the uneatable bitter tubing, roped conduit of gall,

here the gold-celled honeycomb,
and within all the leaved book

recording abominable drama in ship's maw
tragedy of captured and capturer

scenes that seemed to be calling
for overdue acts of conversion.

So the Converter sing

comfort, console, people sold out
dark flesh cargo

drogued in beast state
in the name of cane profit.

Sound myrrh notes to quell
putrefaction's smell.

Cleanse the charnel house
of the bloodbath Atlantic.

Chant new baptismals
for the ones of lost names,

digging song and burial song
for whip, rack, gibbet and chain.

Raise outlaw anthems
to lionheart fight-back.

Coo of the compassion
of Abolition's barbary doves.

Line and sight gratitude psalms,
recite names of resisters,

hoist high notes as guidons
to tramplers of banners of blood.

Divine and cause compunction
skywater to fall.

Scatter grudge clouds
seeding bullet storms.

Hum down vengeance,
call for response reparations.

Summon the wordsmiths,
dancers and artists

singers and players
of instruments must be there.

Honest merchants who follow
the profession of the Prophet.

Blessed be the sowers
and apostles who catch fish.

High Holy ones all charged
to restore legacy of wisdom,

true word ancient
time come, must be fulfilled.

Then balm and anoint
the heads of the young

to call forth and bring in
as yet unknown

fresh revelation and
new moon's understanding.

Even so, is so
the Converter did sing.

Never Expect

Burchell the Baptist
handed you the landpapers.
You were not in a position
to read them, so you call
the name of your place
into the responding wind

by so doing recreating
your ancestral ceremony
of naming. 'Never Expect'
you name your place,
your own spot to cultivate
a small start-over Eden.

Plot for fruit and flowering trees
for your children.
Burying ground for family tombs
and navel strings.
Your strict drawn boundary line
against intruder.

prickle dildo-makka fence
militant as living barbwire.
Begin with one room, piecen it,
fling open your door
or turn your key
when you private.

Build your firewall high.
Raise up your wide barbecue.
Pop loud laugh for peasoup.
Remark openly upon
your ceiling of the sky
and its shifting shade of blue.

Hosanna you build your house.
Yes, Alleluia, you never expect it.

Book

*If Quashee will not honestly aid in bringing-out those sugars, cinnamons and
nobler products of the West-Indian Islands, for the benefit of all mankind, then I
say neither will the Powers permit Quashee to continue growing pumpkins there for
his own lazy benefit... Not a pumpkin, Quashee, not a square yard of soil.*
Thomas Carlyle, *The Nigger Question*

It was bad magic made with pen and ink.
Follow-line soldier-crab hieroglyphics
show off drop-hand scatter mark

employed by Thomas Carlyle to ask
the Nigger Question: Can England afford
to give pumpkin-eating Quashie freedom?

Bookless Quashie had no opportunity
to make said Carlyle guess and spell
how water find way into pumpkin belly.

Freedom comes, Quashie receives nothing
but desires own book to open and sight
read and interpret, revise and analyse.

So beginning from a position of zero
Quashie gathers sundry different papers
that have writing, words and picture.

Part of that letter from Queen Victoria
advising Q to save, and study thrift.
Obscene handbills advertising Q for sale.

Refuses to include verse five Ephesians six
or the hymn of rich man in his castle
poor man at his gate, God made them

every one and ordered their estate.
Q wishes to hear no more about estate.
But includes four bills of lading for cloth

for downpresser, from raw silk to bombazine.
And the paper that claimed that Queen Victoria
has given Quashie, as of first of August, full free.

All this was assembled, impaled and jooked
upon a long spike pointed like Q's story.
And yea verily, that was our first book.

Was It Legba She Met Outside the Coronation Market?

Under the arch of the Coronation Market
she watches the crooked man approach,
he is a dromedary with a double hump,
one of muscle and cartilage, one a crocus bag sack
swollen with the rank weeds and fragrant leaves
of his travelling bush doctor's business.

He bends over and over-looks the child.
She can see the red-veined whites of his eyes,
he leans backward and then falls into a trance
during which he removes his eye's white ball
and swallows it. It reappears in her palm. She returns
the white sphere. he swallows it and speaks prophecy.

Then he limps away with his halt legba walk
but she is left at the crossroads hearing the call,
spirits assembled, casting their lots to decide
who will claim her voice and speak through it
the as yet untold half. Her mother returns, laden down
with ground provisions. The child is silent as the ball's
white weight levitates on the tip of her tongue.

Moonlight City

That Kingston's dungle is called 'Moonlight City'
and Lupus can assume the mask of a butterfly,
that Judas found it necessary to kiss Jesus
is that obstinate beauty's apology for what is vile?

You want eagle's mastery do you bribe D Lawrence
and hitch a broom ride. You see seamstresses living
on pensions earned from stitching up the wounds
you inflicted on the world with your long knives

so you turn and sue your neighbour over property
that is not your own in order to win and spend
what is Caesar's and enter into what you despise –
back door dealings, choke and rob and easy life.

Behold now the peerless flush shade of crimson
blood drawn, mellifluous the betrayer's voice
as he baits you up with gossip hook and line.
But beauty bids you cleanly contemplate the folly

of it all. Discern the shafts of light pointing from
betrayer's knife to blind spirit murderer at his task.
For then he might be led eyeless to gaze
inside, thereby to understand how a landfill

can be called moonlight city, how Iscariot
was must and bound to kiss his friend Christ.
And why Lupus, the wasting spawn of wolves,
can assume the winged mask of butterflies.

Run Greyhound

April dawns in the Ann Arbor Greyhound bus terminal,
a lithe girl tells a man with the locks of a gorgon

how she set out after Jack Kerouac to write a road novel
but her car and craft stalled by the Grand Ole Opry

so she boarded a bus to this station and is awaiting
the coming of her mother who will pilot her home.

He allows as how he has done his travelling in the grape
vineyards of California and the peach groves of Georgia

where he tangled with the law, and ninety days later
'behold, a new man' declares the free-standing gorgon.

Lithe girl presses throat hard to free response, but timely
timely and fortuitously her good mother comes,

blessed turnkey securing prodigal daughter's release.
In unison they refuse offers of help from locked penitent.

Fifteen minutes behind time the silver Greyhound runs in,
gorgon-locks boards with his belongings in a trash bag.

'All these men were released from prison this morning'
whispers a woman accompanying a man with an eye patch.

Riding into the city of Detroit on the convict bus
let the muster now record: one man with a red bandana

muttering steady urgent encouragement to greyhound
to make up the lost fifteen minutes of missing time;

the twin of a bankrupt country and western singer
crooning 'fifteen years, fifteen years of my life

I'm sick and tired of being sick and tired of myself';
whispering woman, 'become your own best friend';

a man, thick cigar store Indian, knuckles of one hand
forming bone buckle at the waist of his pants, says

'imagine I'm the one to make restitution in the sum
of a thousand dollars and attend a turnaround program';

two silent black men in new clothes and Nikes
whom the driver orders to disembark at Wayne.

The bus pulled into their stop. They sat. They did not get up.
The man with the eye patch clutches an x-ray of his head.

The woman beside him insists on whispering. You begin
to make strong supplication along with man in bandana,

for eye-patch is beginning to look like Henry Morgan,
retired wicked buccaneer and born-again governor,

the driver like J Edgar Hoover, the others like Tippu Tip,
Augusto Pinochet, Margaret Thatcher, Émile Zola,

the blood of Cézanne curdling on the nib of his pen.
You make supplication to the swift chariot to run,

you intone 'run greyhound run' as we pass through Indian country
deer fields, where Tecumseh will take us for the long-knife cavalry.

Run greyhound

for leaking caravelles of discovery are upon us, and some
still have just bamboo arrows tipped with cuttlefish bones

and others have mad dogs and fouling pieces, sheep cloning
pox blankets, anthrax warfare, agent orange, blunderbusses.

Go greyhound

press driver press, pedal to the metal to the motor city.
Make up for time lost this day, fifteen minutes, ninety days,

five hundred Babylonian years.

Run, hound of the Pharaohs, run like the twinned Blue Nile
to meet your white same-source branch at Khartoum.

To the city of Detroit where patients discharged from a state
mental hospital clutch sour pillows and wait to take these seats,

where a woman arrayed in scarlet lame chain mail
with a wighat, hirsute visor, overhanging her brow

is slashing out let-live and mercy and forgiveness
where they appear in the text of a creased Bible tract

and two latchkey children lock hands and pipe reed-like
about the impossibility of being separated from their dignity.

In silver tones how they flute, they coo, baby Barbary doves.
Run greyhound run, for they are waiting to board this bus.

Brunetto Latini

And so we proceeded along the built-up mud banking
above a water course like an infernal Bog Walk gorge
with fog draped like wet sheets against fire burning.
Just as how people in foreign build thick mud walls
to keep out big sea when it rises up high and swells
to overflow their food cultivations and pasture lands
in places like British and French Guyana near Brazil.
Or some Italian town named Padua along the Brent
where they erect big retaining walls with weep-holes
to protect tower and yard against deconstruction's
snowmelt, earthrunnings, carrydown and watershed.
It's as if hell's civil engineer got an illegal gully contract
to bitch-up some similar but lean-side walls like that.
By now we are travelling in the bowels of the earth
leaving the murdersuicide woodland so far out of sight
we could not spy it even from the land of look behind.
We buck up a procession of duppies shuffling below
the banking, staring up into our faces like how some
scrutinize one another under the light of a new moon.

Staring, like fast people trying to see who passing by
dark road on a moonless night; staring, like an old tailor
with glaucoma trying hard to thread a fine-eyed needle.
The staring duppies screwed their faces and frowned,
then one sight me, grab me by the hem of my gown
and said, 'Lord have mercy, could this really be true.
Dear poet is it you?' As he touched me I focused hard
riveting my eyes upon the charred skin of his face
so that I summoned up his image from my memory.
And bending near, I peered into his burnt countenance
and groaned, 'Is it you down here so Teacher Brown?'
'O my friend I do hope you will not object if Brownman
turns around and walks along by your side so allowing
this ghostly procession to proceed a while without me.'
Said I, 'I would be most honoured if you and I could sit in,
if it pleases him who is my guide through this dark pit.'
Said Mr. B., 'Whichever one of this done-dead-already band
stops for a moment must remain still for a hundred years,
forbidden to brush off these drops of corrosive acid rain.
No, my good friend, do walk on, I will walk below you
until it will be time for me to rejoin my duppy company
who must perpetually weep and wail in eternal flames.'
So since I dared not descend from my banking and walk
with him on the burning no-life path, I inclined my head,
walked with it bowed low to show my respect, like a mystic
meditating reverently upon the divide between goodness
and evil. 'And what brings you down here before your time?
Was it that big accident up by Providence? And who is he
that is leading you through this dive of such deep darkness?'
Hear me: 'Up there in the land of the living, I went astray,
I lost my livity, lost my way before I reached the fullness
of my years, only yesterday before day did I find myself
and this master here appeared and wheel and turned me
like a Revivalist Darwish/Sufi and is now leading me home.'
Hear him: 'Follow your guiding star, for in all the good life
I experienced I learned this one thing that's true. What is fi
you, can not be un-fi you. And had I lived out my time
and purpose, instead of having it cut short, I would have
helped, supported and encouraged your work, seeing that
you are a true poet, God-blessed. But that bad-minded set,
those pharisaical keepers of our country's gates, whose
hearts are as hard as Blue Mountain alabaster, those who
occupy the chairs of the colonial masters, they envy you

your talent. But poet, the roseapple was not ever meant
to flourish beside these blighted soursop trees, bear in mind
that even old proverbs call them blind-guides, a bad mind
petty, mean spirited, myopic kind; take care to uproot
their grudging ways from your heart. It is written in the stars.
It must surely come to pass that your honours will make
both parties want to claim you. That ram goat will never
reach high enough to crop on such sweet grass, let them
devour their one another's (excuse me) one another's rass.
But never let them cut down any innocent plant that
despite their stunting hands will still thrive amongst them.
'Mr. Brown, if I had my wish,' I said, 'you wouldn't be
banished from the land of the living in which you were
a source of light among our people. I recall your gentle
compassionate and fatherly face as you taught me daily
how human beings can make themselves live eternally.
This image of you, pentimento, surfaces on my heart and
lives on in my mind and while I am alive I give thanks
for it, and I will tell of you to the world through my life
and my art. Your predictions for my future I will file
with some works of mine I save to show a wise someone
who will be the judge of these matters anon, if I can ever
reach her higherheights. As the Most High is my witness
I tell you this: As long as, I say, as long as my conscience
is clear, I am prepared for whatever destiny shall bring
my way. Twice already, I have heard that same prophecy.
But let Fortune's wheel turn around as it pleases, round
and round she must go and countryman must dig with hoe.'
My spirit guide paused when he heard what it was I said,
turned and looked into my eyes and spoke. 'Well heeded
is well heard.' But I did not answer, I went on speaking
to Teacher Brown, asking him who was down here with him
in hell's hot sands, from manor-born to just commerown.
He said, 'It is good to know about some deeds down here
on this walk with me; about the rest of them, let them be.
For our time is too short to engage in idle pointless talk.
Long story short: We were all professionals of true worth,
men and women of letters, scholars of high renown all
brought down by arrogance and excess love of self.
I would tell you more but now I see some fresh steam
rising out of the sand, and some parvenu duppies I want
to avoid are at hand. Hear what I say, don't cry for me or
pity me. Read my books, they vindicate me. In my words

I am alive and I am no duppy.' So saying he turned sprinting
across that fiery plain like a runner competing in a race,
and then he seemed like one who ran ahead and passed
the tape first and not as one who had come in dead last.

from Dante's *Inferno*, Canto XV

To the heirs of low bequests to harvest and glean
abundant sections of favelas and dungles whose evening
fires rise Gehenna-like from cities of waste willed as estate
and inheritance by scavenger foreparents

Because boundaries are in dispute and vultures
draw coal-winged territorial imperative
claiming discoverer status,

the harvesters become wingless predators
with hawk's eyes and cast-iron stomach
of carrion-feasting birds.

They develop internal divining rod and compass
to isolate, assess and detect various degrees
of decomposition,

make rank savoury stew from condemned carcasses
providing the rot has not completely invaded,
penetrated through

to marrow bone, the centre free from corruption.
They feast on unstamped meat, convert the poisons
by the grace of need.

'God of outcasts we ask that you bless this trickle down
repast, sanctify the what-left this day has provided.'

The fabulous sequined brassiere of a rhumba dancer
(in memoriam Margarita) graces an old woman's head,
bright-horned valkyrie crown.

from TRAVELLING MERCIES   45

She strides, ragbag diva, across her elevated garbage
stage, attendant child trails lace camisole of ex-beauty
queen's evening gown.

Dungle children at play prize bent, twisted chassis
of wrecked automobiles and broken bicycles. They ride
reckless, abandoned

along beaten down paths, ragged pennants of jeng-jeng
stream from aerials which no longer receive or send
direct messages.

From crashed car dashboards severed refrains
drip, scores are trapped behind jammed signal bands
of still radios.

Favela and dungle dwellers, children of nothing new
cherish so the mother moon when her full face
brims to overflow

and illuminates by-night excavations. They dig deep
then for items which gleam, washed-over-gold,
semi-precious gemstones,

in hope of finding one or two smooth silver spoons
fallen careless from the mouths of deposed kings,
or a lost, cast-off, golden ring.

For Love of Marpessa Dawn

Long summer vacation 1963.
After seeing *Black Orpheus*
Garth Baker confessed his love
for the gorgeous Marpessa Dawn.

He had been going to Cross Roads
to see her at the State Theatre
and after some seven matinees
and two or so midnight shows

he was convinced that she
was his destiny. As soon as he
finished sixth form he was going
to take a banana boat to Brazil.

Once there, he'd slip past Cerberus
in the form of a massive-headed
wharf dog and find his way to Rio
to meet Marpessa outside a theatre.

There he would serenade her
upon a lute, lyre, or box guitar
with a slow ska, a hard rocksteady,
a sweetie-come-brush-me bossa nova

till she recognized him as Orpheus
returned from the underworld.

And we believed him. We were
willing to make that leap of faith

for we were all misplaced beings,
our true selves ripped from the world book
of myths. But Garth had found his identity
and he would be reunited with Eurydice,

one radiant Marpessa Dawn.

Miles in Berlin

Siberian winds
held him hard
up against the east wall
but rudeboy broke free,
ripped off Joseph's coat
and rode west.
You're in the aisle seat
every seam leaking
dark light. Granite love
urging you to drink from
the crystal skull
sacrificial bowl.
But your refusal to imbibe
is another rhyme.
This was Miles.
Prince of horn come to charm
you out of yoke and bit.
Kind of Blue, Time After Time
he piped till all your strained
seams split and let fall
long water, vital heartwash.

The Garden of St. Michael in the Seven-Hilled City of Bamberg

I believe St. Michael to be my friend. He the broadsword
wielding warrior commander and captain of the righteous
host and army. I saw him once in profile, just a glimpse,
limned in the pitch dark of the stone garden where the mad
serpent-heart bull-body was trying hard to swallow me.

In the name of 'woman no cry' St. Michael manifested
and trashed him like a common pickpocket. But he asked
me never again to speak of it. Nor of all his other victories
angelic and chivalric. I intend to keep these acts secret.
He's asked me to tell you instead about his garden.

For that is what St. Michael does, he gardens to unwind
from vanquishing the host of the global bad mind.
He has drawn up a plan on the ceiling of his chapel
in the seven-hilled city of Bamberg, chosen plants
he has admitted into the garden flourishing in heaven.

In the cultivated beds grow the lavender, the evergreen,
lilies arum, of the valley and white, gentians, cowslips,
Turk's head cactus and mint, camomile and castor oil,
foodkind in the garden aye pregnant pumpkins, pears, apples,
tomatoes and corn, cleansing aloes for cathartic purposes,

and tobacco to calm. Here I'm asking him to consider
a sunny corner of his garden for a few plants Jamaican
like the sansivira or donkey's ear, the low-ranking
periwinkle, aka ram-goat-dash-along, because the Christ
rode upon a donkey to go and become holy scapegoat.

And because it is written how the poor, the contrite
and cleansed are blessed, the inclusion of poor man's
orchid, Job's tears and the cerasee would seem to be
fitting, in-order and completely appropriate. And good
saint gardener Michael, let there be roses upon roses.

I am weary of all winters mother

I fear I will stop strangers
in the snowbanked street
to confide 'my mother is dead.'

By Borders on Ash Wednesday
a white-haired woman wears
an ash cross on her forehead.

I am weary of all winters mother,
winter within, winter without
strict-fast Ramadan, Lenten do-without.

Invitations From Heathcliff

The blessed Jessye Norman at morning
the keening Kathleen Battle each night

that is how she endures the ice age
with its freezings, exactness, deferrals.

January to May, regular doses of spirituals.
And Heathcliff has been sending her messages

scripted in code on cedar chips. Sharp cedar
scent of his cologne, cedar, the tree of coffins.

Can you not see she is dying in this winter
while you work away and send messages?

Here she is wearing a long hot-pink dress
with a floating sheer fringed black scarf.

She has bought and paid for carioca shoes,
all her long legs want to do now is dance;

and present, attentive, Heathcliff knows this.
Coffin biter has been sending her messages,

maps marked with the best place for trysts
and costly night show tickets to the Follies.

Poor Mrs. Lot

And so it was that Lot's hard-ears wife
became a pillar of solid eye water.

Poor woman, frozen there crystalline
up from ground, salt stalagmite.

One last glance at what you left behind:
your mother's cutlery, your yellow plates.

One more look behind to memorize
the lay, the order of the landscape.

The red water tank. The church spire.
One last look is enough to petrify.

Like you, she should have cried
as she left, not daring to look back,

savouring hard homeground with salt.

Natal Song

I come to find my vital self left back here
so that I land in Xamayca with quest fever
and all the while Africa you had my remedy,
my baraka in your mouth, so that even
when they split and redirected your course
my name remained a seed under your tongue.

Khakibos and lantana spray us with green
shrapnel as we plunge through the Natal bush
this Sunday in search of the sleeping rhino.
Rendra riding shotgun displays a mandala
drawn for him by the wild Tuareg, Awad,
a black ink seal against Indonesian dungeons.

We debate upon the possible effectiveness
of a paper charm to ward off Suharto,
then all conclude that maybe a bush bath
of khakibos might do as well since it repels
insects and possibly all crawling pestilence.
So we progress through the Sunday sleeping bush.

Near here a lion ripped life from a woman's throat,
but for us the wildebeests descend from cave walls.
They are now proceeding in an undulating charge
across the high veldt, underhides gleam through
sparse pelt hairs. Marvel that this wild woman
has lived to see the running of the wildebeests.

Buck, eland and antelope all now crouch down
under the smite of midday southern Africa sun.
An equestrian black and white striped convention
conferences beneath writhing acacia trees, and Clare
reveals how the first task of the newborn zebra calf
is to memorize its mother's unique schizoid makeup.

We call upon the elevated and figured giraffe,
its sandpaper tongue swiftly negotiating round
thorns plaited into the tender foliage at the crown
of trees, city stories high. In the high lion-coloured
grass sit two females with necks like obelisks,
horns and ears imitate intricate Nubian knots.

Continent of my foremothers, to reach back I have
crossed over seas, oceans, seven-sourced rivers.
Under my heartbeat is where you pitched and lodged
persistent memory, rhythm box with no off-switch,
my drumbeat and monitor which never let me
settle for barracoon, barracks, camp or pagoda.

The veldt resounds with the ringing hammer
upon anvil cry of the fiery blacksmith plover.
All the time source was remedy for quest fever,
for the lion at your birth straddled your sign,
sacrificed appropriate sheep and beat back dogs
designating your song as the bleat of scapegoat.

Now the pride of even stricter lion demands
the total banishment of the captured within,
the scour and disinfection of mental barracoon,
the break and burial of old iron. Nothing less.
If you rise up full grown, assent and embrace,
will lion open your throat and silence, or lionize?

Thank you God for this day most amazing. Amen
good driver Adrian. Tomorrow I will drink bush tea
on the Island of Salt, realizing that we never
did see the rhino. But the wicked toe of the ostrich
excavated a stone with the seal of a mother and child
upon it. Kenzurida found it; and Africa, I kept it.

Over the Island of Salt

Journal Entry:
Before dawn we land
on Ilha do Sal
the airport lounge
under a fluorescent sun
blooms orange socialist chairs
like rows of hibiscus.

Ilha do Sal. That is where for three dollars U.S.
you buy a cup of bush tea such as you'd receive
in the house of a humble Jamaican person.
You purchase too a perfume sold under the slogan
'Life is best lived without a plan.'

You've watched him go under every time the waves rise.
You shout from the shore reminding him how
you are his lifeguard, mender, mincer with elastoplast
arms. But he dives deeper. What to do, what a life.

You board the plane for the high veldt where hyenas
laugh at humanity, and the bush falls green in winter.
You too will howl at the moon over Africa.

You could have turned that tank around and kept going
through lion country, but you are too old for such folly.

Besides, you can only sleep if diving one is beside you.
You can lie still on a presbyterian bed narrow as the straight
road to heaven. You fit tongue and groove, dovetailed corners
of armoires. That is your way.

Don't send any more messages. The last one said
'there is a place here for you.' That is a ruse.
There is no place for us, neither in lamb nor lion country.

On Ilha do Sal you buy bush tea, you leave. Live your life
perfumed with no plan. Return, ask the deep diving one
how are things in the ocean?

Song of the Scapegoat

The goat's head lies now so still
eyelashes sealed in flyblown sleep
short bone shanks crossed at rest
splintered broken drumsticks over
basin's rim. Only its body is missing.

They are selling it in halves in another part
of Victoria's market. The goat's head is red
with wet curls, behold the obliging smile.
It lay its head on the block so sinners
could lay their sins on its back and then
in gratitude drive it into the desert

there to meekly sound a lambent goodbye
as they slit its throat and skin its hide
and stretch it seamless into a public drum.
Lion says those days are done, let each one sacrifice
themselves, let everyone now pay for their own sin.
Let there be no more sell-out of the scapegoat
in any half or part of Victoria's market.

Shining One

You'd be able to tell this fellow,
he shine like new money.
                     August Wilson

I engaged the finder man
the seller of pots and pans
to search for you for me.

I paid him good money,
sold my gold guard ring
(it was protecting nothing).

I gave finder man the proceeds
and said, 'go find my shining man.'
The walkabout never did return.

After centuries I settled for
a succession of mattesomeones,
but religiously when dark season

came on, I would want for shining.
To finder man, seller of pots and pans
I had given this basic description:

'Look for the one with big clean hands
and the soulcase that is transparent.'

I lost my money, forfeited the fee,
the errant locator never did return.
But one day, a Sunday, in January

I sighted what appeared to be a bonfire
in my garden, for the flame of the forest,
the japanese lanterns and the candlewood

were hot ablaze and the late poinsettia
leapt like flambeaux at the gateway.
I ran downstairs in my nightgown

to investigate this garden arson
and I saw you there, lost in wonder
at my full bloom conflagration.

Shining man, radiant, let finder man
keep the money from the gold ring.
Enter, come burnish my life, my being.

To Absorb the Green

To endure the strict days of ice and winter
come absorb the green of December grass
that the egrets bring. Silk cotton blossoming.

Sunday morning waters reflect lozenge light
and dark green foliage; a thousand leaf nuances.
Do not leave Xamayca forever, your wild self

sprouts here like long-limbed guinea grass
dispersed, blown about and tossed, seeded first
off the Guinea Coast. You are African star grass.

Settle lightly, moved by breath of unknowing.
The egrets perch upon the trees like birds,
blossoms of birds, or white-feathered flowers.

Medicine Bundle of a Blackfoot Woman

If this medicine bundle tends to remind you
of a delicacy duckonoo, a tie-leaf parcel wrapped
in banana leaf or trash,

know that it contains more than cornmeal
or red-skinned potato sweet and steamed.
It holds within cures,

the stuff of dreams and antidotes for ridding
you of the effects of evil eye. I have been
making it for years.

A medicine woman of the Blackfoot Nation
told me how to start it with a root shaped
like a clean heart.

She told me to bundle it and pray sincerely
for goodness, kindness, and mercy to follow
me. In time I added

such things I found as I trod through earth,
things to heal the effects of slip and fall down.
Righteous rosemary,

the navel string of my son, my mother's last look
(she looked like a bride), her countenance washed
and clarified

the essence of sincerity and hard-to-cultivate
forgiveness. How can that hold in it you ask?
And I say don't worry about it.

It's my medicine bundle, don't it?

Her body became a container for stars

After, her body became a container for stars.
Some nights when the room would go dark
she would feel the movement of the sun's cars
burning her bare soles with traction marks,
racing upwards on the red rush of her blood
via capillaries arteries and veins till they emerged
from her rib cage and triumphantly parked
beside the hunter with his jewelled girdle
and his dog, guarding the live ruby of her heart.
Outside her, the three sisters and pilot moons
would be braiding her hair and anointing her feet,
and what others took for wind-zephyring tunes
was really the call and response of the Pleiades
singing sweet constellations in her sleep.

Studio I
Brother Everald Brown

An elder, an artist, a Rastafarian
who dwells upon Murray Mountain
St. Ann, where springs the lambs' bread
colly. He paints the dreamscapes alive
behind his locks, Ethiopian Coptic scenery,
multiple mountains and fallow clouds
inclined to rain down angels. Sometimes
he shapes pregnant-bellied instruments
which breed cosmic sounds for Egyptian
winds to zither across their strings.

Studio II
Seymour L.

The winter after she left him
he made pictures of flying women,
line drawings of long-tressed
lithe comely women in flight
often heading over the Hudson
leaving just their trunks and legs
to remain in the composition.
Some faceless ones would enter
head first into the chaste square
of Arches paper. Half in half out,
constructed to always be without
his complete vision and framing.

Studio III
Petrona Morrison

rises early and raises tall shrines
fills clay cups with spirit palm wine
salvages the remains of charred cities
and rests them on beds of fragrant leaves.
Bring the symbols of hard life come,
bring the gunmetal, barbwire and bomb
and watch her bend them into shapes
which encircle and reconnect.

Studio IV
Barrington Watson

There is a woman lying on a bed
spread with zinc white sheets,
a boychild on a chamberpot throne
in a twilight room.
The countenance of the boy
is that of a child well fed
on slow-boiled cornmeal porridge
which luminizes the skin.
The woman looks pensive.
Outside the canvas stands
another son, a master
who immortalized
his own dark mother
with a nod to Whistler.

Cézanne After Émile Zola

Émile, your friend from childhood
turned his pen and drew your blood,
created a character with your features
and cast him as an artist manqué
of coarse peasant's dress and rude speech,
a suicide with no sugar for his morning tea
whose vision was crazy, cracked impasto.

When they belittled you, the them
who in the end do not count or matter,
your blood ran choleric. What camp follower
can ever see far? But when Émile
cut you so, your blood became acid, vitriol,
green gall. Solitary you painted Mont Sainte-Victoire
over and over until you drew and coloured
a hard mountain range for a heart.

The sky breaks in unblended strokes,
the stones in your landscapes separate.
The features of the perpetual bathers
become gross. Constantly you wash
the memorystain of first friendship
before Zola's achievement in Paris.
Over and over you recreate boy's memory
of friendship carried by clean streams.

Praises in Papine Market

You stand in Papine market three years to the day of your
    mother's death

and marvel at the sight of fifty-seven bottles of coconut oil
    gleaming, longnecked,

and count as many of St. Thomas logwood honey, making you
    want to chant 'Glory'

for the sight of earth bounty, blessed be the green country
    yielding this food.

Weight of ground provision, cornucopia of fruit. Sugarloaf
    pineapple old lady sells,

says the small hole in it was drilled by woodpecker's beak
    because mango season finish.

Of the hole too in heart-fruit, drilled long, drilled deep, how
    come some seed time

and lie-fallow last so long? Why some water diligently and is
    chaff they reap?

You don't know the answer, just sing slow and hold to the
    rosewater flesh of naseberry,

chant OM like bees in logwood thicket, blessing selling in the
    market.

Crossover Griot

The jump-ship Irishman
who took that Guinea girl
would croon when rum
anointed his tongue.

And she left to mind
first mulatta child
would go end of day
to ululate by the bay.

'I am O'Rahilly' he croons.
She moans 'since them
carry me from Guinea
me can't go home'

Of crossover griot
they want to ask
how all this come about?
To no known answer.

Still they ask her
why you chant so?
And why she turn poet
not even she know.

Petition to the Magdalen

I

Eight days before my birthday is when
they celebrate your saint's day.
Did you ever see the four candles
I lit in your high church
in Toronto one winter?

You never speak to me.
I have never seen you in a dream
except for my Egyptian alabaster jar
which I like to think contained
spikenard for anointment

and my great capacity
for weeping maundy tears
enough to wash face, hands and feet.
You never associate with me
who, like you, wasted my love so

while waiting for the one
who could tell me all I ever did.
But you never speak to me,
Magdalena, even when I went
to the desert and lived in your cave.

You only left messages,
cryptic petroglyphs, but one day
you caused my shadow self to separate
from me, took me from behind myself
like Augustine.

I never met him at the well.
Perhaps it would take too long to tell
all that I ever did.
It was my heart he went after,
took it from my chest
while I slept late and careless,
washed it in well water,
woke and ordered me
to the desert to wander.

Gave me a water song to sing
even as I wandered thirsting
with you as my absent patron saint.

Alabaster jar for anointing.
Costly spikenard.
Capacity for tears enough
to wash feet
hands and hearts.

I came after you to the tomb
but He was already gone.
Magdalena will you come
to me

now that my mother
can make for me
on spot intercession?
And did you
accept the four
candle flames,

indulgences I purchased
for my son my mother
my true friend and me?
And could you just appear
now, saint of wild women,
in a dream?

II

Magdalena,
you know that story
the one where Jesus
did not ascend into heaven
but survived crucifixion
and you and he settled down
and raised children?

I doubt its veracity.
Let's face it Magdalena,
some women are not the kind
that men marry.

They are love's substitute nurses
who draw venom
from men's veins,
and swab and stitch
eviscerated egos.

Manpride thrown down
in soiled laundry,
they refresh in the well
of Samaritan ministry.

That the son of man
honoured you is a good story,
that he knew all you ever did

but loved you still,
that he considered himself
blessed to take
a woman experienced as wife.

A woman tender and capable
of washing his feet with her tears,
of drying them with her hair,
of bearing it out beyond doom,
of arriving there before
the Easter sunrise to balm
his murdered self with spices.

The sisters of your first order
are working still,
The piece of papyrus
detailing the end
of your story is lost.
But Magdalena, loyal follower,
'dear friend,' what was the true end
of your story?

Iron Shirt

I'm gonna put on a iron shirt
and chase satan out of earth.
Maxie Romeo

Respect due to the man who would chant
that song. The same man wandered
about the hot streets of Kingston
wearing nothing but a gash red wound,
open wound he received when Shaitan
took molten scissors to his iron shirt,
cut his well-intentioned armour off
and told the third world knight
to take a walk.

It is 3 a.m. You wake from beside
your beloved who rode through snows
to join you. You loved so, then lay down
to sleep and that is when goddamned Shaitan
comes in through dream gates to seed
fear images.

Beneficent watchman who never sleeps,
see how this freezing night has driven
duppy and daemons indoors to leech
on light and lovespirit. Cold-blooded
creatures, spirit tramps want now
to burn bad lamps.

There is no place here for them to pitch
these malevolent leather-winged spirits.
Not here, not now.
Watchman, drive all wretched
from this house.

My Island Like a Swimming Turtle

My island like
a swimming turtle
surfaces in the fishtank
of the television

black rubber tire smoke
belching from its breath
and machete chops
and gunshots on its carapace.

We suck our turtle children
unformed out of our eggs
and boil and boil ourselves
in vicious mannish water.

Our bigman fat posse
eat beef Wellington
even on Ben Johnson day.
Feastdays, we suck salt.

War correspondents
come with seeing eye
cameras to show dirty
turtle laundry to the world,

how our big sea fishermen
cannot swim.

Cry out O terrapin.

Questions for Marcus Mosiah Garvey

And did prophets ascended come swift
to attend you at the end
in your small cold water room in London?

Was it William Blake now seraph and ferryman
who rowed you across the Thames to where Africans
took you by longboat home?

And did the Nazarene walking upon water
come alongside to bless and assure you that he
of all prophets understood and knew

just how they had betrayed and ill-used you?
And did you wonder again what manner of people
sell out prophets for silver and food?

Lush

Perhaps if you remain you will become civilized,
detached, refined, your words pruned of lush.
Lush is an indictment in this lean place
where all things thin are judged best.
What to do then with the bush and jungle
sprouting from your pen?

The dream house at Enfield where you received
poet's schooling. House with slightly cultivated garden
bearing black-eye and congo peas beside English roses.
Loose curled heads of lettuce sheltered under yam hills
red-pulp oxheart tomato tethered to quicksticks
of unhemmed tearaway fence

round the yard's swing-skirt circumference.
Japanese lanterns threatening to raze coffin wood
of tall rank cedar tree. And beneath it a running
river babbling deep water glossolalia in spate,
summoning the shy river mumma to appear.
By a full moon you can read by, she would coil

her fish half on a smooth rock, and comb and
comb her long water-wave hair. Cain and Abel
lived in the village. When Abel was slaughtered
Miss Jamaica paraded his head on a sceptre
as she rode in her win-at-all costs motorcade.
From his blood sprung a sharp reproach bush

which drops karma fruit upon sleeping policemen
to remind them of their grease-palm sins of omission.
A bordello replaced a butchershop in the tidy square
and St. Martin de Porres became the village Patron Saint.
I could go on, but I won't. My point is finished, made.
May lush remain the way of my world.

Bam Chi Chi Lala

It is fall again, October rains
and red trees signal you
are entering change season.
Your guinea blood courses fierce
and you think to drink gold leaf
in a camel bid to store sun.
See how your small boy
has become a fine man.

You cross the street to bless brides
and cross yourself as ambulances shriek by.
This morning you woke at five and kept
company with the monk of Gethsemane,
lauds and aubades. In Hanover your people's
river swells because the hurricanes
have wept and flashed their epileptic
selves across the West Indies.

How do wild spirits gain entrance
into humans?
Do they make their way through body
orifices as we sleep?
If that is so then it is best to say
the sealing prayer before slumber.
'Lord, please keep all demons away
from the nine gates of my body.'

Or better still, forsake shuteye,
join the night watch and patrol
the border country between
the worlds of sleep and wake.

Do small deeds of love for the world.
Remove traps and tripping stones
set by the wicked for the weak.
With the aid of clean mirrors
bring the lost from behind themselves.
And then pass silent by graveyards
taverns and public cotton trees where
the ambitious hold duppy conventions.

Aye, earth's garments wear so heavy.
See how much the queen's robe sags,
trimmed as it is with feathers of the vain,
sleek ermine and jewels of bright ambition.
Be wary miss monarch of the ones who come
ostensibly to admire the intricate inlaid
workmanship of your throne, for they
may be measuring your neck's length like

Queen Mary the pretender, whom some
toasted with wine glass on top of glass of water
because they said the real monarch lived over
the ocean. No one crowned her that is true,
she is a pretender just like you, save for this
one thing. The first word
you read spelled your vocation, Singer.

If they knew how all ambition
should come to this, autonomy
autonomy over the me myself.
Sovereign over self kingdom
feel free whomsoever to fight over
the cold food Babylon has left over.
Bam chi chi lala
angels dance rocksteady
on the head of a common pin.

Softly now
our Beloved
is convening
pleasant Sunday evening.

from

Controlling the Silver

Island Aubade

One bright morning when my work is over,
I will fly away home.
                    Traditional Jamaican

Before day morning, at cockcrow and firstlight,
our island is washed by the sea which has been
cleaning itself down with foamweed and sponge.

Fishermen who toiled all night and caught trash
let down their seines again on the off chance.
The never-get-weary-yet cast off and their nets

will break from abundance. On land, the feeding
trees or kotch-hotels of egrets, bird-bush lodges,
start to empty of perch occupants flown in pursuit

of proverb's worm. The faithful night watchman
will punch the clock and so end dark night's shift.
He earns the right to strike a match, light first fire

and issue out a sheer blue smoke scarf to morning.
She will catch and tie up her hair with this token,
gunman and thief slip and slide home with long bags.

And the farmer turns in the sleep that is sweet,
a laboring man sleep that, he'll flex his wrists
in practice for machete wielding; and the woman

will give suckle to a drowsing infant. In the field,
the low of cows in need of milking ministrations.
The jalousies of the choir mistress, who sleeps alone,

open as she raises a revival hymn over the yard
to hail the coming of our Lady of Second Chance,
the Mother of Morning who invites all visitors.

★

Come drink this cup of Blue Mountain coffee
stirred with a brown suede stick of cinnamon.
Just say no thanks, what you need is bush tea.

Pumpkin seeds parched, steeped in enamel pot
with kept-secret, fitted lid, so no steam escapes
before you raise its doctor-vapor to your face.

Thank source, she will insist, for the mysterious way
spirit debones from troubled flesh, easing you
from sickbed across entrenched ice and tundra

up the seven thousand feet peak of Blue Mountains.
Startover is where Mother Morning lives. By leaven
of struggle-up mantra, return Shulamite to Xamayca.

Morning has become my mother, bringer of curing
bush tea. She is now mother to the whole island,
grandmother to Miles, mountain born, who thought

'Maw'nin' was a lady. 'Show her to me' said my son,
and we pointed him to a rose dawn over our village.
Above our house was Blue Mountain Inn, the Queen

of England dined there, we did too, till hurricane
raised high the roof. She comes bringing frangipani
and jasmine commingling in a clay jar of terra cotta,

cloth cotta on her head coiled to bear, asking where
we want these bride-ivory flowers dew-drenched
from wedding nights. Set them on the Singer machine

by the door of a concrete-nog cottage where wrote
the penkeeper of Enfield. Chalk-white walls scripted
with calligraphy of ivy, acid-wash, slate roof porous

in parts, board latches to doors and windows gaped
wide so as to allow loquacious choirs of gospelling
redthroat birds to chorus in the brick floor kitchen,

where I stood over a gas stove and stirred, porridge
for my boychild, for his dog, cornmeal and beef bones.
Stirred, till we arranged ourselves as migrating birds.

Emulate the fit fruit that mother of morning brings, mark
June plum's defensive seed, so deep the purple skin
concealing the milk-flesh of most private starapple

(which Miles consumed only in twos). She always has
the same greeting, our lady of second chance morning.
Hear her: 'my children, come in like the new moon.'

If we encounter turn-back northers and land after noon,
she will be pleased to fix us second breakfasts of cooked
food. Sweet potatoes, medallions struck from yellow yams,

unfertilized ground provisions we'll eat seated under
poinciana trees, which drip petals, like scotch bonnet
peppers, capsicum benediction on our second breakfast.

Don't shake hands with the wicked, eat greens, abase
and abound. After this, no one you'll meet is a stranger,
she'll say, and give you a mesh fan of flexible ferns.

For this Jamaica sunhot is hell on your skin, burnt raw
by radium. Going to bathe in the family river cousin,
we need to go back to where our people come from.

Dear Cousin

i

We might not reach in time to de-ice you
into renew. You lie in the foothills

of Calgary and I'd like to be able
to tell you that the azure harbor ahead

is the horseshoe of Lucea Bay, but those
white horses run too fierce.

You have the eye, from the foothills you can
discern the washed bones of many million

drowned on the Atlantic side,
where long-meter waves hexameter swell:

Wild horse, mounted militia, martial law
search and destroy, thundering buffalo,
bull bucker, overseer, guineagogue,
badlove-takelife waves, gathering brute force
to draw you under, come girl, wash your heart,
with heart-rinse of machete-split coconut.

ii

They packed you in ice early up north
where you plied your wordsmith's trade,
rubbing the salve of convince on dry tongues
which became then sure and swift of speech.

Your own tongue aches from tip to root;
you want to assuage it with water coconut,
for killer crab and that low grey lizard
beneath the water jar have harmed you.

When at age seven our two eyes made four,
you were my first cousin who taught me
how a river named by our generations
was benign, would not harm, but pull and haul,

bank to bank safety. You said to me, sit there
on the grave stones town girl, sit and learn
how to discern between one good duppy
and a bad one. Under the damp, dirt cellar

of the Harvey house we exhumed porcelain
bowl shards, buttons of bone, blank-stare dolls
with decayed bodies, and nacred spoons we used
as earth-moving tools for finding Harvey roots.

Excavating

the long line of David and Margaret,
disinterring evidence of the stillborn
who did not draw breath at begetting time.

Which begins with Nana Frances Duhaney of Guinea
and William Henry Harvey of England, who wed
and begat Tom, Fanny, Mary and David
Harvey, he who wed Margaret, progeny

of Leanna Sinclair also of Guinea and George O'Brian
Wilson of Ireland. This is how we come to come from
the long-lived line of David and Margaret,
who begat Cleodine, Howard, Edmund,

Alberta, Flavius, Edmund, Rose, Doris
and Ann. And I am from Doris, and Joan
she was from Ann, but it was like we were
daughters of one woman. Come in cousin

from the cold: there are times a one has to
seek succor under own vine and fig leaf.
Let us look now to the rock and quarry
out of which our generations were hewed.

Ode to the Watchman

As we exit from the old city before day
we sight the night watchman at his post,

evidence of his vigilance against nocturnal
furies red in his eyeballs. He did not bow

though, no, not him, it is right to thank him.
All praise to you O beneficent watchman

for keeping guard over us while we slept,
blessed be your eyelids which did not blink

even once in solidarity with those lowered
shutters, window blinds and jalousies.

You remained awake, ever alert, armed,
with only your night-stick, rod, and staff,

your aged, cross mongrel dog rampant
at your side, even as the smoke pennant

blown from your rough-cut filterless
hand-rolled cigarettes flew out full staff.

For pushing against that grease-stained
tarpaulin of despair and not allowing it

to befoul us during our needed night rest.
For keeping at bay restless rolling calves,

trampling down from those sleep hills,
busted old rusty chains rattling to shake

the firm resolve of small hearts, thanks
watchie for keeping them from breaking

and entering our little children's dreams.
And now kind watchman go home to rest,

you who did not seize and beat the beloved
as she roamed the streets, composing the Song

of Solomon. Go home now good watchman.
The last hot rush of caffeine pins that pricked

your blood awake has been rained from your
thermos flask, your bread-back of night lunch

cast upon the keep-up fire in your belly. Cease
the anti-lullaby you keen to maintain wake,

the sun is here to take your place.

Our Ancestral Dwellings

Columned cotton trees are our ancestral dwellings.
Beneath them stand the departed who missed
the return voyage on redemption's longboats.

Cravers of salt, gravalitious warriors enlisted
in world wars of must-have; stirred-up ones
with unfinished business who cannot lie quiet.

Necessary guides, who without warning occupy
the skins of fervent women, commandeering
prayers to sound earthquake and storm warnings.

Undelivered orphan children seeking rebirth,
engorged navel strings in need of clean-cut,
for only then can they die and come in again.

These are ones congregated at cotton tree root,
some offering themselves for hire as if alive.
Others limbo there till moved by hosts to depart.

We have no business here. Drive past.

The Wandering Jew and the Arab Merchant
on the Island of Allspice

Along the road we passed the wandering Jew
in his dark suit, his cart piled with dry goods.
Further along, we sighted the Arab merchant,
his wares rising from his back in a camel hump.

Attar of roses, good for your noses, come to you
from me and Moses. Buy your perfume pressed
from those fragrant rose blossoms of Lebanon.
All the way along the Damascus road, the Jew

has come to sell his things to the freed Africans.
The Arab came following the long spice route
to this island of Allspice. Shalom and Salaam
becomes 'Sallo' on the tongues of the Africans.

They were known those days to find themselves,
the Arab and the Jew, in the same free village,
on the same day, peddling their similar wares.
And in the village square they would sit at noon

under the broad shade of old Lignum Vitae trees
and break bread together, unbraid Challah, share
aish or Syrian bread. Aish, ancient name for both
bread and humanity. They'd sit, eat and remark

how some hard-pay Africans do not like to part
with silver, and how they both dread the walk
through cockpit country. The Arab gave the Jew
a chip from the ka'ba to protect him in the valley

of the shadow. The Jew gave the Arab an amulet
shaped like Moses' tablet. To the Africans, they sell
Bibles, then all bless Father Abraham, before taking
to hill and gully roads across this island of Allspice.

Passing the Grace Vessels of Calabash

Our foreparents carved on
(lest they forget) maps, totems
symbols and secret names,

creating art when some
would claim we existed
in beast state.

Every negro in slavery days
had their own
hand-engraved calabash.

So they'd drink water from
grace vessels, their lips
kissing lines of maps

leading back to Africa,
to villages where relatives
waited for years

before they destroyed
the cooking pots
of the ones who crossed.

So Who Was the Mother of Jamaican Art?

She was the first nameless woman who created
images of her children sold away from her.
She suspended those wood babies from a rope
round her neck, before she ate she fed them,
touched bits of pounded yam and plantains
to sealed lips; always urged them to sip water.
She carved them of heartwood, teeth and nails
her first tools, later she wielded a blunt blade.
Her spit cleaned face and limbs, the pitch oil
of her skin burnished. When the woodworms
bored into their bellies, she warmed castor oil;
they purged. She learned her art by breaking
hard rockstones. She did not sign her work.

Jah the Baptist

for the Rastafari Elders

Children call the fruits of locust trees, stinking
toe. Are they what John the Baptist fed on?

In those Bible stories our mothers read to us,
John the Baptist was dread righteous Rastaman,

trodding wild in the desert, feeding on honey
and locusts, 'herbs for my wine, honey for my strong drink.'

Balancing acrid with sweet of wild bees, he invoked
brimstone, lightning and fire on generations of vipers.

Flee, he warned, from Babylonian standards. Play not
by the rules of their game, for they detest the dark

of your skin, the thick of your lips, the wool of your hair.
Strive not to imitate Babylon, become your own man and woman.

Before he baptized with the waters of clear insight,
hard-case words of locust musk kicked off his tongue.

Poison Crab

That bunch of corroded keys
dropped in your lap, now hangs
deadweight on your days.

In morphine sleep you dream
by the bottle-torch moonlight
of village children, owners
of the roads in crab season.

Crack backs underfoot
sever limb from limb
snap those antenna eyes
scoop articulated parts

into long bags hauled home
to boiling pot. They stiffen
before yielding up flake-flesh
to scourge of hot pepper,

bow broad forehead
to strike-down of hammer.
But always there are ones
that bite back and do not let go,

till thunder roll.

Fool-Fool Rose is Leaving Labor-in-Vain Savannah

Grass cultivation upon roof top
hot sun striking it down to chaff,
Rose bundling with strong effort
scorched fodder fit for Jackass.

Rose securing sinkhole in river
with rock salt and rose quartz,
to find favor with headmaster
inspecting her morning tea sugar.

Sign on sign and she did not heed,
returning to shut-bosom mountain
spite river's mouth spitting weeds.
Open lands with not enough room

for her to raise a modest Rose tattoo.
Soothsayers in their suits well-pressed
prophesying Rose-death from fatigue,
expecting a legacy of marrow secrets

scrolled soft-tubed in yielding bones.
A quiet stranger came empty handed
to the well; Fool-Fool Rose offered up
her cup, in thanks he uttered key words

that turned her from housetop agriculture,
and locked off her ambition to bottom
and dam a river hole. Farewell/hosanna,
Fool-Fool Rose is leaving Labor-in-Vain Savannah.

Rainstorm is Weeping
An Arawak Folk Tale Revisited

The weeping Rainstorm from our reading book
bore strong resemblance to Aunt Cleodine.
Her full head of hair whipping up great shocks
of black rain clouds, her tall body wedged
between heaven and earth's birth passage,
and rainfall her eye-water on storm days.
She craved power, Rainstorm, for here it said
in the reading book she trained her hard gaze
at those installed on clouds, and made her way
to exalted places to sweep them out by force.
Sadly, she got stuck between sky and earth,
the reason she weeps, and why flood rains fall
Octobers and most Mays. And when she rails,
she invokes the levelling hurricanes.

Aunt Alberta

Amazing how Aunt Alberta was named by an act
of sheer prescience after a Province of Canada. Alberta
born 1903 on the island of Jamaica,

one Easter morning cracked an egg and sighted a ship
becalmed between yolk and albumen. Taking a hint,
she boarded a steamer and sailed

faraway from life in a sun-lit green Jamaican village
founded by her grandfather into a city of ice storms.
No lingua franca but the tongue

of Quebecois, and unaccustomed hard labor in Mont Royal.
She lived in service, taking orders; a saint remitting
money and care-parcels for an entire village.

Photographs show her dolorous in snow banks, solitary
in deep sylvan glades of photo studios, till at aged forty-
four she married one Geoffrey Seal,

a Barbadian, himself stone-faced in service, first and only
man to uncover her loveliness. It came unexpected,
Aunt Alberta's late luck, in the form

of a tender companion who wore her wool scarves
like prayer shawls, holy her barely-scented handkerchiefs.
He slept, telling her pearls like a rosary.

Aunt Rose

Our favorite photograph shows her in a blush-pink
Parisian spring suit. Observe the soft felt cloche,
the high-heeled shoes, tendrils of suede straps
x-ing across insteps, kissing her long narrow feet.

Damask Rose, too gorgeous, reduced sincere men
to silence. They'd end up drumming nervous digits
on taut throat-skins, attempting to tap out wooing
messages, appropriate toasts to the Rose of Sharon.

Even in Montreal, where gilded French women
would go, exalted by haute couture, she'd cause
Quebecois men to groan 'mon dieu' and plunge off
street cars calling 'comment s'appelle Mam'selle?'

Beauty concentrated, top to base note she trailed.
A human pomander, the very particles and waves
of her roseate self would scent odorless atoms.
Her essence permeating skin, blood, bones, flesh,

she drew in breath and blew out rosewater scent.
Fragrance-deficient ones begged caresses from her
scented hands which in the end became coated
with attar of Roses. Attar yes, Rose knew burnings,

but the fair Rose of Jericho, never wanting to speak
of such scorchings, would press down her torched
voicebox, scarred and keloid with beauty burns,
to the last releasing rose scents, but no sounds.

The Burden Bearer

My sister Carmen's hair uncombed
sprouts like fronds of the palm tree.
When the fits take her, she convulses
like a palm tree in hurricane season.

'I am the burden bearer,' she moans
as she spasms, foams and falls, assuming
position of family scapegoat come to bear
for all, one hard bitter-gall life of battering.

The one with sores no blue-stone cures.
The one with scorch blister of the brain.
She who is designated to carry the weight
of our people's communal sin burden.

My sister does not bear silent, she stirs
word-salads of poems, badwords, psalms.
She's learned by heart most of King James's
Bible, she wields its language as weapon.

Yea verily the Bible says honor thy mother
and thy father, but parents provoke ye not
your children to wrath! She curses my mother
for the fall from a vehicle while carrying her.

For the deep cut to her brain which festers
and erupts, testing our house's foundation.
Job-like she wants answers to hard questions.
Out of all my parents' nine children, why her?

Hosay

After warm rains the West Indian ebony lifts its arms
and salaams blossoms. Stop the car and join the Hosay.

On their indentureship he steered them straight
to the West Indies: these Indians come in bond to Cane.

Hosay, Hosein, East Indians delight in offering praises
to their Spirit Guide, the son-in-law of the Prophet.

He their one kind overseer in the mud-sop of rice fields,
Hosein himself would weed rice and root turmeric.

Benevolent master he bestowed on them great gifts;
so the African Jamaicans would one day come to believe

'Indians get talent to drive truck and catch fish.'

He their present Patron Saint revisited Jesus' miracles
and charmed the fresh fish of la mar into wide nets.

Instructor Hosein is who taught them to steer
the prosperity path away from cutdown razor grass.

In thanks each year they construct for him a marvellous
multi-colored house, and hosay across the Savannah.

Creation Story
Why Our Island is Shaped Like a Turtle

On the Shell gas station map, Jamaica,
big-up and large over broad Caribbean sea.

The pin head of our village turns up and pricks
your finger so a drop of blood spots Harvey River.

We're really on the map now you say, then wonder
why our island is shaped like a swimming turtle.

A possible explanation:

Swimming turtle smitten with hot sun
paddles up from water bottom in search
of light become her love object.

Turtle call is ska beat, turtle tail licks
riddim, tail of turtle, nine miles long
forms sea-side of Negril.

Turtle implores Creator, leave me here.
I choose to fall from heaven under
the water to be with hotsun.

So creator strikes turtle with stick,
her shell cracks, in rush big rivers,
hills and high mountains swell up.

Turtle strikes bargain with Creator
to remain above water, housing Taino,
Europe, Africa, India, Asia and China

just to be with sun, and tell the world
that Jah Mek Ya, so Jah said, Yah.

These Three Butterflies and One Bird We Interpret as Signs

i
Historis Odius Odius

Leave earth Nymphalid,
soar and stay bourne within
spirit breath, doctor breeze's
reviving, bearing currents.

Do not pitch now or pause
to malinger over sugar mill's
whatleft, trickledown leak,
or lick blackstrap molasses.

Avoid caprice breezeblow
or any old batterbruise fruit.
To feast on over-fermentation
makes you white-rum drunken.

Keep the pace, this trajectory
will take you to fat-leaved
feeding trees, far from poison pin
and trap net, fly on, hard fi dead.

ii
Tiger Swallowtails

When fully grown, Tiger Swallowtails
have swift roaming flight patterns.
Their unprepossessing caterpillars
are not much to look at, resembling
droppings of dull-plumaged birds.
But despite their crap appearance
they persist in arching themselves
to feed from chalice-petalled tulips,
till one day they lift out of pupa state,
flashing their V-shaped markings
and at wing-tip, topaz tiger's eyes.

Urania

Truth is, you are really moth's blood relative.
But unlike your Cuban cousins, you do not flock
to the seaside with escape rafts, or show any
predilection whatsoever for sea grape,
cocoloba.

And on account of your formal appearance,
dark velvet dress with transverse bands
of ruddy gold paved with powdered gems,
some say you are swallowtailed butterfly
which you are not.

For often in winter before tourists arrive
you're found taking sun under mangroves,
confounding lepidopterists claiming to be
your superiors and most learned colleagues.
So they believe.

And then the Bird Banana Katy

These green gold hands
checked by tallyman
hefted by broad-back
gave you your name, Katy
bird, go eat of them.

Last night we stopped
at a hotel for dinner;
a white-jacket waiter
stripped one naked,
doused it in cane liquor,
and set it on fire. Katy
it blazed like a cane field.

Behind every bush
lurked an African
determined to return
to Igboland or Guinea.
Shadows danced macabre
on terrace walls.

Hibiscus oozed
blood wounds
crickets chafed
hind legs
beat wings
riot riddims.

Surf pounded
like wardrums.

Burnt sugar
seared the air

red-jacket waiters marched,
marched like militia.

Today we'll just
drive on and chew
on the rose-heart
of the good guava.
Fly over there Katy,
and feed on your banana.

Don C and the Goldman Posse

We drive past Discovery Bay
and conjecture how Columbus may
have heard of this rumor about
Jamaica once being part of Atlantis.

Don C and the goldman posse
arrived by leaky caravelle taxi,
and barely make it to the beach,
and as dem reach so, dem start
with the hold down and take way.

Buy out the bar with counterfeit.
Eat off the bammy and roast fish.
Turn round and wipe-out Arawak
with pillage, plunder, and disease.

Hours beat, the Don C posse leave
because no gold was really on here,
except for that let off by the sunset
into the sea, which makes small boys
leap over white limestone cliffs for it.

Where the Flora of Our Village Came From

Credit the Spaniards with introducing sugar cane
plus the hypocrite machete that cuts both ways:
Columbus encouraged Arawak to grasp the blade
of his keen sword even as he smiled a greeting.

Pindar nut, Cherimoya and Alamanda – stowaways
from South America. Ipanema girl Bougainvillea,
since she land, has been in one extra Miss Jamaica
contest with Poinciana, Madagascar hottie hottie.

For mangoes and pungent ginger, thank East Indies.
For jackfruit and the high-strung chattering pod
wind-activated, christened by someone acquainted
with carry-go-bring-come, the woman's tongue.

Courtly bowing Bamboo came calling via Hispaniola.
Mother of chocolate cocoa, is Polynesian Gauguin girl.
The silk pulp of Chinese hibiscus, crushed, blacks shoes,
and zen-like bleeds to ink for penniless school children.

Coffee, kola, ackee, yams, okra, plantain, guinea grass,
tamarind seeds and herbs of language to flavor English;
those germinated under our tongues and were cultured
within our intestines during the time of forced crossings.

By the Light of a Jamaican Moon

A tongue-bath of moon.
And your countenance
is glazed.

This compelling force
draws you to it,
inclines your face
and silvers it with kisses.

Catch is, your face is turned.

Your desire
for moonlife
raised like sea level.

You tidal pool,
and dryland dwellers
wake and find you
watersource in their midst.

You are not sure
how you reached,
but you let them drink.

You can read by the light
of a Jamaican moon, so we read.

Lessons Learned from the Royal Primer

for Velma Pollard

Taught us how Bombo lived in the Congo
in a round grass hut. Bombo was the boy
who sported a white cloth about his loins,
causing one of our linguists to conjecture
that perhaps Bombo's rough garment gave
the name to one of Jamaica's curse-cloths.

Now we were never told exactly what
that little boy Bombo was doing, except
just dwelling as a dark Congolese native
in his round-domed grass ancestral hut,
supported by a thorny center pole. But
what the Royal Primer forgot to tell us

was this. It seemed that it was the king
of Belgium who gave strict instructions
to his soldiers to cleanly chop off both
the little boy Bombo's hands, on account
of the fact that balls of rubber cultivated
by Bombo were deemed too lightweight
and not enough for the needs of Leopold.

Hirfa of Egypt

Guess who I met up with in Egypt? Hirfa,
in a souk, over a glass of mint tea.
She informed me through an interpreter
she did not know that she had been featured
with a stink camel in Royal Primer
and that they'd made her look ridiculous.
(That book made Giza's pyramids seem small.)
Hirfa said that she was no Camel Girl,
vowed she'd wear no lattice-eyed burqua.
That she'd study under Hapshepsut,
iconoclast, female Pharoah and Queen.
Hirfa is now revisioning herself,
with a lion's body crouched to leap
and with a woman's head uplifted.

What of Tuktoo the Little Eskimo?

Whose father sawed round holes in the ice
and dropped his rawhide line baited
with bloody gut from previous catch
and hauled large pearl-scaled fish up,
then dipped icy fish flesh in cool seal oil
and filleting its fishmeat with a bone knife
fed it to each of his many children in turn.
Fish being brain food made Tuktoo wise,
he became a cinematographer and recorded
the Inuit's true ways through fish-eye lens,
an epic named Atanarjuat the fast runner.

Arctic, Antarctic, Atlantic, Pacific, Indian Ocean

The world's waters rolled into a chant, we learned
the oceans by rote and song. Arctic began with 'a'
drawnout and soon the crowded class would rock
back and forth on wooden benches packed close.
With a low moan, is how Arctic started. Along came
an ant, and Arctic became Antarctic, body of water
that left us cold, until we reached Atlantic. Then
we suffered sea change, and would call out across
the currents of hot air, our small bodies borrowed
by the long drowned; Atlantic, as if wooden pegs
were forced between our lips; Atlantic, as teacher's
strap whipped the rows on, to learn this lesson
Arctic, Antarctic, Atlantic, Pacific and then Indian.

Louis Galdy of the World's Once Wickedest City

*He (Galdy) set up as a merchant in a modest way, but soon found his fingers in
many pies – merchandise, shipping ventures, produce dealing, the slave trade...*
                                                              Clinton V. Black

As blond, black-skinned sailor pickney scrambled
down back alleys warbling 'you done
dead already' Galdy would just shamble
through the ruined town of Port Royal stunned.
In the wake of the fall of Christendom's
wickedest domain, some power spared
him to tell the tale. What had he seen down
when earth engorged him? Inferno maybe.
Cut-throat, scurvy sea dogs, doused in white rum,
become torch men in sea of molten goldpiece.
Bawling badmen waving letters of marque
and asientos, Galdy just went quiet.
After earth swallowed then spat him to sea,
he ceased the buy and sell of human beings.

Black Like This?

To the girl in the great house who cried
as her nurse bathed her
'If you touch me I might turn black'

some questions:

Black as decay signalling
seek cure, cut-out, abandon?
Black like trick-light of raven
revealing what in you is broken?

Jet like johncrow absorbing
collective curse and rejection,
swallowing carrion, keeping
the corruptible kingdom clean?

Black as night's courtly love
for light, keeping her at days end
under the wideness of his tent,
delivering her virgin to the world?

Black like deep shelter-holes
where stars go to expire, hiding
the lost-cause of their falling?

Black like that you mean?

River Mumma

She sits with her back to us, her teased hair
is now bleached platinum. She has affixed
paillettes of rhinestones and sequins over
her shimmering scaled skin (here we have
a perfect example of how to gild a lily).

Please tell the River Mumma we are here,
outside the doors of her underwater clinic.
We say this to nurse souls rolling bandages
and grinding medicine bluestone in mortars.

Though we see how her hairstyle has changed
(it used to dip so evenly in regular waves),
and we see her lips are stained parrot-fish red
and her hobble skirt is bling-bling iridescent,

we still bring her this serious crab bite case
who is in need of her specialist treatment
(hair of dog; water cure for bite of crab),
for maybe River Mumma medicine can cure her.

We bring a wedge of brown soap for cleansing,
a lost wedding ring found, to make payment.
Details of one fraudulent agreement we seek
to bleed indelible ink from, Mumma please come.

All the while the drowned souls drape bandages
in long white strips across the clinic's entrance.
Deaf to us, the drowned ones pound bluestone
in mortar pestles. We are not acknowledged.

The River Mumma Wants Out

You can't hear? Everything here is changing.
The bullrushes on the river banks now want
to be palms in the Kings's garden. (What king?)

The river is ostriching into the sand.
Is that not obvious? the nurse souls ask.
You can't take a hint? You can't read a sign?

Mumma no longer wants to be guardian
of our waters. She wants to be Big Mumma,
dancehall queen of the greater Caribbean.

She no longer wants to dispense clean water
to baptize and cleanse (at least not gratis).
She does not give a damn about polluted

Kingston Harbour. She must expose her fish
torso, rock the dance fans, go on tour overseas,
go clubbing with P. Diddy, experience snow,

shop in those underground multiplex malls,
spending her strong dollars. Go away, she will
not be seeing you, for you have no insurance.

The Wisdom of Cousin Fool-Fool Rose

Two middle-aged mermaids who got soaked,
we re-enter the village running the gauntlet
of the relatives calling: Morning cousin this,
Morning cousin that. Morning cousin from foreign.
You hear the news, cousin from across the water?
Our dear cousin Fool-Fool Rose is on-dying.

In her one room, prostrate on her single bed,
the red gold and green headscarf worn off
for the first time in must be fifty years;
her locks like wool serpents scroll Aramaic
script across the tablet of her white pillow.

We ask her:

Cousin Fool-Fool Rose,
how do you bear the spite of death,
old hige, bitch, long in claw and tooth,
rip and chewing flesh to dry bone?

She smiles and points to a calabash gourd
netted. A red, green and gold crocheted reticule.

I and I sight that bag there? When death fling pain
the I open I mouth wide and swallow, then spit.
When it full, the I fling the bag over I right shoulder.

Such wisdom the I learned when the I sight up
the quiet stranger by the well. The gift
of I cup, the pure intentions of I heart
was enough to set I on the path to wisdom.

The I departed from Labour-in-Vain Savannah,
and went to dwell instead on the road to Heartease,
among the likeminded who defend peace,
who labor only to mend the tear-up world.

For the record, the I was never a one who walked
ten steps behind any Kingman. The I never sight up
to become downtrodden. The I became instead
handmaid of wisdom of the order of Grandy Nanny.

Look through the window and sight that cloud,
floating cotton mattress or a level-vibes carpet,
as how I and I feel to call it. The I tie the mouth of this bag
and then the I mount upon that flying carpet cloud

with this bag full of beating, and the I ride.
I and I and I am kin, through the line of Guinea woman.
I and I and I come from generations of horsewoman.
How I and I bear death's slings and arrows? I and I ride.

The I can sight up from the way I and I look soak-up
that I and I penetrate below, seeking for an answer
from River Mumma. But the old order is passing
and things are not the same beneath the river.

But why I and I go there for? No true wisdom seeker
should ever depend on that sometimeish spirit,
that uncivil servant of Babylon who should retire.
Verily the Kingdom has not removed, it is still within.
To get the wisdom the I seek, I and I must cleanse.

Wash face, hands and feet, rinse out hard-ears, and pass
clean wet hand (benediction) over the crown of the head
thus reopening the mole (fontanelle). I and I will become

once again as an innocent. Then get flat on the ground
and beg the Most High, entreat the Most High for help.

The cleansing of the feet, face, hands and crown,
the thorough washing out of the channel of audition,
is a vital move, for I and I like that obedient little youth
to hear and say 'speak Lord, for thy servant heareth.'

The bag is full, the cloud is here, the I must mount the flying carpet
which lifts the I out of the range of death stabs aimed at the I flesh.
The I destination is Heartease; but to reach there, the I must ride.

In the Field of Broken Pots

Water goblet, bitter cup or monkey jar.
Know that each of us has been part of one
of the above; and that in time we're bound
to become broken down into small shards.

In a vision that night River Mumma came
and grudgingly dispensed to you a pill of clay.
You swallowed it, then lay down and joined
the vast deposits of like returned to ground.

You said: that was my answer, but I don't want
to go yet. You said:

In a West African village, on the day I depart,
women will gather my clay pots in the field
where the vessels of all departed are smashed
so that the dead are never equal to the living.

The plain terra cotta rounded cooking pot
patterned with my daughter's palm print,
the goblet I glazed with crushed gems, then
sketched on with thorns, will all be broken.

Only weaver birds, and ants who sip raindrops
from shards, will ever drink again from my pots.

O weaver birds and ants who drink of raindrops
promise you will come as guests to sip of my pots.

But I May Be Reborn as Keke

Keke, piece of broken clay pot
used now as base to start new pot,
culture of clay that went to fire
and returned to function as talisman,
keystone, sure-fire foundation
of new water jar; made the age-old
walk around way. Coiling the rolls
to make cool water hold in smooth
checked monkey jar. Keke, old heart
of used pot, cast back on wood fire
but flame proof this time, sure guide
of new jar, shard of which will become
in time, keke, most kneaded clay.

Change If You Must Just Change Slow

We will crouch down then in a red earth
hollow, press our lips close to the heart
of this deep Cockpit Country and call out
please don't change or change if you must
just change slow. Old countryman riding
jackass, big woman watering the dry peas,
fat cow, and mawga dog, one-room dwelling
with intricate carved lace fretwork eaves.
Heaped yam hills, garlands of green vines,
cockades of bamboo on crown of the hillside.
Little bit a country village place or woodland
name of Content, Wire Fence, Stetin, Allsides,
far from domain of gunman and town strife.
Country we leave from to go and make life.

The Yard Man
An Election Poem

When bullet wood trees bear,
the whole yard dreads fallout
from lethal yellow stone fruit.

And the yard man will press
the steel blade of a machete
to the trunk, in effort to control

its furious firing. He will dash
coarse salt at its roots to cut
the boil of leaves, try slashing

the bark so it will bleed itself
to stillness. And yet it will shoot
until the groundcover is acrid

coffin color, the branches dry
bones. Under the leaves it lives,
poverty's turned-down image:

blind, naked, one hand behind,
one before. The yard's first Busha
was overseer who could afford

to cultivate poverty's lean image.
But this yard man says since we
are already poor in spirit, fire for it.

Controlling the Silver

For Thou, O God, hast proved us:
thou hast tried us, as silver is tried.
Psalm 66

Her silver-money necklace and bracelets
made agreement with the wind that went
like this: if she rode upon her gray mule,
seabreeze would kiss and coins protest, creole music.

Silver coinage; England minted, soldered
into flexible chains then freely draped
about the neck and wrists of our Guinea
great grandmother: controller of silver.

Let us praise now market women: higglers,
who maintain our solid, hidden economy
in soft money banks between full breasts.
Gold next; now these women control silver.

In those Sunday markets across the island
the sold Africans would gather, ostensibly
to sell their ground provisions, cultivated
at the end of long days in service to cane.

In what-left hours, they transformed rock
hillsides to bearing ground under the shine
eye moon, which is why ground provisions
gleam when tumpa knives cut them open.

Let us praise now artisans and craftworkers,
builders of Empire. Skilled ones who raised
up temples of marble. Masons and carpenters
constructing suffering into stone and fretwork.

Dovetailers of joints denied benefit of all union.
Hail O basket weavers, potters, calabash carvers,
seamstresses of garments stitched from ripped-
off ends of regulation oznaburg; skilled recyclers

of missus' old clothes. Bush doctors, gatherers
of curing herbs. Hawkers of vengeful potions,
Myalists, Pocomania and Revival practitioners.
New World Christians remaking massa's religion.

Praise to those gathered in common markets,
redemption grounds where Africans swapped
blood secrets, kept spirit, passed on information
about insurrections, and bought and sold silver.

So the silversmiths developed a brisk trade
in bracelets and guard rings; the thrifty bury it
to dig up one day and buy freedom. The silver
likes market culture, stays there, does not leave.

Deep shut-pans of silver lie buried at tree root.
On moonless nights you may walk by coin-light,
if your good foot happens to kick loose a lid
a source of pent-up shining will be released.

Crocus bags of silver still banked beneath
banana trash mattress (we should look for it).
Draw of silver passing from hand to hand
in a susu/partner (you must pay the banker).

One day the coinage runs so hot it runs out.
The Governor has to be told that if he dies
that night with his two eyes wide open, there
might be no silver coins to keep them closed.

Not a threepence, a sixpence, not one florin.
No metal-alloyed between the stirring notes.
Not even a lion-pon-it shilling to connect
one pound to guinea, absent all the silver,

except for that revolving around the body
of our women like Jupiter's multiple moons,
plunging between black mountains of bosom
into drawstring vaults of calico threadbags.

These women accustomed to Guinea gold,
these people late of Benin, now control silver.
Enough to buy land, even to lend to massa,
every coin a cocoa, filling up their baskets.

Full baskets of Redemption Ground Market.
Bob Marley's muse followed him home
from there, when he went as country boy
to buy raw cow's milk, and two yard fowls.

By day a market, by night hallowed ground.
The workplace of productive angel bands
and anointed spirit guides with real power
in the blood to wheel you free from crosses.

Wheel you till take-set spirits stagger back.
'I was a smoker, I was a drinker, a backslider,
God see and know I was a thief, till the Holy
Spirit collar me, and spin me like Ezekiel's wheel.'

Praise to the power of our Guinea woman great-
grandmother, higgler with pencil in her tiehead
to cancel old debts, seamstress with the scissors
in her right hand who will cut for us fit pattern.

Nana who can balm you clean in five bush bath.
Big woman, who can afford to pay Peter a shutpan
of silver as indulgence for your soul. Mercy agent
seated astride her grey mule, come to ride you home.

Making Life

Jah never run no wire fence
Bob Marley

The cherry afterglow of Negril spring break,
sunset rays knit into his tam from the gold
ball dropped behind Rick's cafe,

my student oversteps a gray snowbank
on Liberty to ask me 'Lorna, how can you
live in exile?'

Because it would take too long to tell
how I left because my Jamaica was like
a faceman lover

with too many other women he was seeing
on the side and I might have just died
waiting for him

to finally get round to doing right by me.
But that is too long a story, so I wander
and wonder instead:

is it because we came from a continent
why we can't settle on our islands?

Did our recrossing begin with deportation
of maroons to Liberia via Nova Scotia?

Are we all trying to work our way back
to Africa? For soon as we fought free

we the West Indians picked up foot
and set out over wide waters, to Cuba

and Panama, anywhere in the Americas.
And we never call ourselves exiles.

We see our sojournings as 'making life.'
So after world wars when they wanted

souls to bury dead and raise near-dead,
they called us in as duppy conquerors.

But when the job was done, they then
tried to exorcise our task force,

but we remained, took their brickbats
and became Blackbrits and Jamericans.

I first came north to paint pictures, but
maybe I wanted firsthand acquaintance

with the fanciful places named in songs.
Isle of Joy, the song said Manhattan was.

I'm from island in the sun, I had to come
and my sweetheart poetry joined me.

Not really exiled you see: just making life.

Your Ice Art, Michigan

Across the wide snow-primed canvas you paint
with vegetable, mineral, water and oil medium,

there are skeletal groves of charcoal stick trees,
put-to-bed fields and high rise totems which

accept salt sacrifice thrown at their feet. Except
for blocks of primary color barns, your palette

is toned down with frost tempera. When you draw
ribbons of skim-milk rivers, you loop and loop them

till they connect with Superior's waters, then burst
into true blue in exuberant recognition of source.

Admiration for your perfect composition laid down.
Bands of roads run straight and across, intersect

then part. So effective your ice art that some days
I have no need to favor green. Still, I remain,

expectant witness to your up-from-tomb spring.

Broadview

for John Edward

Take the red streetcar that stops at Broadview
you will come to a sealed lane named Brydale
by walking along wool weaver's avenue.
On the corner in a tall rented place
with stained-glass cathedral windows live now
two people whose lives add up to over
a century. Two who took a late chance
to mend and solder their divided selves
into strong binding two-toned interlace.
Torches carried became welding flames

for trying days; briar ways they came
through acres long untended. At ease then,
scythe rank choke weed, lower the nightshades,
sweet thyme take root in perfumed herb garden.

Missing the Goat

Here we create new rituals, fill a crystal
goblet with dried redbud drawn sorrel
purchased late this December snow day
from Chinese Trini in Kensington Market.

À votre santé with drink so wine-alike,
gingered, spiced, hybridized wassail cup
the jewel juice of Xamaycan hospitality
raised to this our first joined Christmas.

For the feast we had planned a portion
of curried goat accompanying a turkey.
But the host of yardies peopling this city
came before us, got all goat and have gone.

Even the papershod, halal-butchered ones
plunging from Greek meat shop windows,
Esther Williams in a dive on the Danforth,
are now bought, sold and gone everyone.

Does mass exodus of sacrificial goats mean
the first-comers will have days of plenty
and we late sleepers mere fowl flesh? No,
in season of wine on the lees and marrowfat,

we'll feast then on curried some-other-flesh.
Raise our crystal goblets garnet with sorrel
to Advent arrivals and small constellations
of now beneficent stars over our night rest.

The Crying Philosopher and the Laughing Philosopher

inspired by a Rembrandt etching

The Crying Philosopher

For 99 days this city has been covered with snow.
Today will make 100 days since the streets
have been under deep cover. All snowfall metaphors
are officially exhausted. No seraph's eiderdown
torn, no celestial beer-head foam from Valhalla
mead mug. This is bully-boy and bitch-spite snow
in attack mode and treacherous. In origin pristine,
at last state become soiled, lowlife, gutter fodder.

The Laughing Philosopher

All is for tomb-rending time when the white garden
revives, full color. This chill blanket shields bulbs
and forsythia. Rhododendrons, wheat and azaleas
need downtime under ice cover. Chaste monk's hood,
indigo, iris, and provence lavender require annual dye
of blue ice water. Dead then awake, ground water table
risen so high the faithful walking, come April, on water.

Hard Food

Decked in her finery, Doris would transport
every specie of provender. Opting to jettison
her own garments when the scales registered
outrage, scandalized, horrendous overweight.
Not one finger of green banana surrendered.

She journeyed to see her sisters Rose and Ann,
her suitcases fat with the food of their Hanover
childhood. In advance, she'd hunt and gather
Lucea, white and yellow yams, sweet potatoes,
and cassava, green, Bombay and Julie mangoes.

Sheated in the obituary pages of newspapers,
they landed ripe, fit for sucked-dry endings.
So they read, they ate, sure of finding at least
one soul known to them in the death columns.
'See a Duhaney dead here, she must be related

to grandmother Nana.' Bliss is a ripe Julie mango.
'Wear Pimento grains in your socks for heat.'
'Mama where you get that kind of foolishness?'
She never said. My mother, possessor of esoteric
information, boss of things strange and arcane,

packed sugar cane next to aloes and tamarind.
Foil-wrapped escoveitched fish like silver slippers.
'When I land, I'll cook for them. We will feast
whole night till morning.' On my way to Calgary
with a bag of hard food, mother I've become you.

Rites

Past the Drumheller badlands and Sylvan Lake
the shaman came at dawn by way of Red Deer
and made for the Foothills, where he rattled bones
in a bladder pouch, built fire in a smudge pot
and washed her in sweet grass smoke, to no avail.

And if special rights could have been transferred
for me to become a Blackfoot medicine woman
skilled in the use of puff balls to stem hemorrhage
and the administration of mind-clearing bullberries
beaten off branches just after the fall frost, had I been

made honorary Blood or Piegan dancer in a jingle dress
trimmed with copper tinkling cones to sound scatter
for crabs, I would have doctored and danced. Instead
I stood by the window and watched her go the way
of great female buffaloes at Head-Smashed-In-Jump,

those matriarchal leaders of herds with wild bangs
of coarse black hair and dowager humps she and I
dreaded we'd inherit. 'We thought we had more time,'
reads a caption in an exhibition on Plains Indians
at the Glenbow Museum. We thought we had more time.

Aunt Ann

Ann Rebecca, bird of paradise,
is that you grey-owl watchful
among clay plots of Mount Royal
Cemetery where your washbelly
last child resides, sent off by her
own girl in a drizzle of red roses?

Ann Rebecca, are you dark-eyed
from presiding over new grave?
In watch and pray mode do you
pilgrim go, through Côte de Neiges'
streets each night trumpeting
down stone walls and iron gates
to enter and protect your charge
confined now to a narrow bed?

Does morning find you unseeing
by windows, dear Ann Rebecca?
Accept, aunt, a jar of dead-sea salts.
Anoint it under heart, massage
its brine savor over your chest.
Caress the place you first detected
her infant heart-beat, there she is,
connected. The lovely are passing.

The Liberator Speaks

Down the avenue of Ficus trees
with overlapping braided roots,
late-rising blackbirds carry news
from eaves of cool blue buildings
housing ministries, to the sea side.

They fly over bands of school girls
in sheer white stockings, who sing
as lush memorial wreathes are laid
at the stone bust of Benito Juarez.

And there to the right of Benito
stands Simon Bolivar, The Liberator.
Ascetic, watchful from extended vigil,
listening for Spain's imperial knock
come to lead him away blindfolded.

Ah, the sweet levitation of Spanish.
Language held, clipped, then loosed
so that those Habaneros who claim
its custody, can question the tongue
of these other Spaniards of San Juan.

Simon Bolivar would sometimes
turn to the nubile Jamaican girl,
daily bearer of his midday meal
wrapped in a clean linen cloth,
breast of dove. Turn and bid her

listen as he spoke his liberation
plans in strong creolized Castilian.
The liberator confiding fervently
aired out detailed secret schemes
to a young still-spirit African girl

silent as obsidian. When he stopped
she then rose, adjusted her skirts,
collected her empty mahogany tray
and departed. Plans for the liberation
of the Americas bound in her braids.

At the Keswick Museum

Amidst the packhorse bells, cockfighting spurs,
the glass walls of stuffed birds, and a giant set
of cordierate impregnated stones which sound
to create an early form of xylophone, it stands.

The wooden chest you are asked to handle
with care, for it houses the 500-year-old cat.
Its concave eye sockets still scoop darkness.

In those days darkness was on the whole land:
take for example in the parish of Lampligh
in 1658, the following deaths were recorded.

Three frightened to death by fairies.
Four perished from being bewitched.
One old woman put to death for maybe
bewitching the four just mentioned.
One poor soul led to unfortunate end
by a will o' the wisp carrying her wide.

In addition, educated people in Lampligh
claimed their domiciles were inhabited
by bogies, spirits and dobbies (duppies).
A dobby or duppy it seems, was or is
an household spirit which can get mean
and vicious if not hospitably received.

So there in the pastoral Lake District
the good people found it was necessary
to root frightspirit rowan trees by gates,
and to place oddly shaped, waterworn stones
(preferably those with a single eye-hole
representing the all-seeing adder) atop walls.

Eye of adders to ward off witches, bogeys,
dobbies, all categories of malevolent spirits,
including nightmares, which were steeds
ridden by witches like the one put to death
for taking the life those four souls. So when
they took her life, her cat gave up his ninth.
That's it there petrified in that wooden chest.
Cross yourself and just back away from it.

Bam Chi Chi La La
London, 1969

i

Calm as a Coromantyn warrior baring his chest
to the branding iron, this man was standing outside
a corner Lyons in January, wearing a thin floral shirt.
One helluvabitch cold tore at the hibiscus over his heart.
So he unbuttoned button after button until almost
barechested, he stood calm as a coromantyn warrior
giving it up dry-eyed to the white hot branding iron.

ii

In Jamaica she was a teacher. Here, she is charwoman
at night in the West End. She eats a cold midnight meal
carried from home and is careful to expunge her spice
trail with Dettol. She sings 'Jerusalem' to herself and
recites the Romantic poets as she mops hallways and
scours toilets, dreaming the while of her retirement
mansion in Mandeville she is building brick by brick.

Apollo Double Bill

Those parrot fish men in pimp regalia,
red light red to bottom of the barrel blue,
issued forth from whale-sized cadillacs
sliding soles of dyed alligator skin shoes
across the slick pavements of One Hundred
and Twenty-Fifth Street and Lennox Avenue.

Whatever you do
don't ever make eye contact with a New Yorker

because they might be packing.

'Now,' said he, 'you wouldn't just happen to be
some of them girls who when singers come on
start screaming and shouting now would you?'
Enquiring man clad in head-to-foot red,
with gold teeth ample to light up stage,
wants to know.

So my friends and I, all full-of-mouth,
fine-feathered, turned out for hot fun
in the summertime, stare him in the eye
and backanswer, 'what's that to you?'
'Cause if you are,' he says, unlocking
his red rib cage to release a steel shape
that shifted to his hand.

'I'll be forced to take my forty-five and silence you.'

Not a peep from us as we sat, wings dropped.
Till we slipped to the fowl roost where unchecked
whoops and whistles, pillow-fight feathers flew.
This was after all the 'Sock It To Me Summer'
double bill with Junior Walker and his All Stars
plus the sweet-boy Smokey Robinson. What could
any young girl in Summertime do but scream?

For all the music, New York: Hugh Masekela at the Village Gate,
Arthur Prysock in Central Park, James Brown at the Apollo,
Les McCann at the Bottom Line. In nineteen hundred and sixty
eight inside Sam Goodys on Broadway, John Coltrane blew
and split open the bark of my young green Tamarind heart.

Guernica

On the third day I went with Seymour Leichman
to the Museum of Modern Art, there to see Picasso's
Guernica, and the woman bearing a lit lamp burst
through the casement at the upper left-hand corner
of the canvas; the disemboweled horse screamed.
Swift sleight of hand; Basque woman dropped fire
in the niche Coltrane split with the lip of his horn.

Turpentine top notes, base notes of linseed oil; scent
of painters' studios can cause salt to wash my eyes.
It was originally my ambition (that is why I'd come)
to become a maker of most marvellous pictures.

So I apprenticed for a time in the studio of Brachman,
and then under master painter Jacob Lawrence. Great man.
Don't look to right or left, just do the work, do the work.
Slip past those petty guards at the Metropolitan's gates
who'll seek to dispatch you on their fool's errands and
do the work good, Jacob said, just do, and do the work.

Catch me running with that city rhythm. Up in the morning,
take bus to the train, take train to West Fifty-Seventh Street
to the Art Students League. After classes take the A train
to filing job on Wall Street. File, then take train to Greenwich
Village, there to cashier at the Rugoff's Fifth Avenue Cinema
between Twelfth and Thirteenth. So train and paint and train

and file and train and cashier and so see the second half
of a movie. I saw the body of work of Akira Kurosawa
in parts. Swords of Seven Samurai, claw-foot of Throne
of Blood, round about midnight, rode the night train home.

Winter vespers in a Village church, I offered up prayers
to St. Jude, invoking as litany a Beatles song. Home came
the boys in body bags to be replaced with fresh live ones.
I am that I am, and I am beauty, intoned the Black people.

Imagine if you can, the entire population of Jamaica
can be accommodated on Rhode Island; and my first
white Christmas spent alone in a Queen's apartment.

Here is a secret I learned from experience: there is
a finite number of times that one can descend into
a New York subway. Should you exceed or overstep
your ride-quota, the New Lots train will station itself
in your head. To be rid of its iron-squat, you must
get brain washes in warm Caribbean sea water, or
you'll sit by Grand Central station and weep, or fall
off at Brooklyn's last exit. I confess: I looked behind
as I left, the wide sky over the Hudson was burning.

I Buy My Son a Reed

All day, John Coltrane invoking a Love Supreme,
woke up with him. In the slumber days before
the why of the reed's insistence shook me

I'd play H. Mann's Battle Hymn, soft beginning,
Shams of Tabriz asking Rumi sly trick questions,
near the end all the entire reed bed is keening.

I buy my son a reed instrument, for Shams,
in thanks for the days I woke in charnel house
unconscious, yet here I am, relating this tale.

He does not touch the reed, wanting to postpone
the must and bound day when said instrument
will function as straight extension of his breath.

Let's say now he will not. Leave it, I too slept late.
Today here's John Coltrane, who desired to become
a saint; his giant steps shook down sheets of sound

to wrap and seal off heart's core. I was twelve
when I heard someone say his lungs contained
air enough to move large rooms. May my son's.

I Saw Charles Mingus

There went Mingus, high as he was wide,
moving stately galleon up fifth avenue.
Tall valkyrie-blonde woman heartside,
they changed sides, crossed over
on approaching the New School. It was cold.
How did I see Charles Mingus pass?
I cashiered at Rugoff's Fifth Avenue
between Twelfth and Thirteenth Street
after classes at the Art Students League.
One extra A train token busted my budget.
But you don't want to hear that; to you
I'm an island upstart, allowed in through
tradesperson's entrance. True that, but
point is I did see Mingus, walking. As I
cashiered, Master Akira Kurosawa reeled.